The Wrong Side of History

A Satirical Synopsis During Troubled Times

By Robert Keough

Copyright ©2020, Robert Keough

All rights reserved. No part of this book may be reproduced or utilized in any form or by any means, electronic or mechanical, including photocopying, recording, or by any informational storage and retrieval system, without the express written permission from the publisher except for the use of brief quotations in a book review.

www.marlowinc.com

Printed in the United States of America
First Printing, 2020
ISBN 978-0-578-74676-0

To Kirsten.

It will get better.

Luv, Bob.

The Wrong Side of History's
INTRODUCTION

By the time you read these words, this book may be out of date.

It's the summer of 2020. Plague and protest are in the air, both literally and figuratively. Good people, causing *Good Trouble*, are fighting the good fight as they struggle against forces that are constantly reminding us why we can't have such nice things as life, liberty & the pursuit of happiness.

The enemy? An offshoot of humanity we shall call *Homo Brutalis*. Mean, cruel, barbaric creatures holding the planet hostage, wielding such weapons as greed, violence and racism, augmented by anti-science dumbfuckery & hypocritical fundamentalism. They look like us, at times act like us, but their motives are harmful, selfish, deplorable, murderous ...Republican.

These braying, belligerent bullies have been with us for a very long time. You know them. You've seen them. You've met them. Chances are, you're related to a few of them (Will you *please* stop sending us those *emails*, Uncle Billy)! *Homo Brutalis* thrives off of social chaos, pain, suffering, divisiveness, and "owning the Libs."

It appears these vulgarians may be at a point in their *evolution* - ironic since they don't believe in Darwin's theory - where they're overexposed, exhausted, having finally played out their gnarled hands in this screwed-up card game of existence. It would be best for our global society if this harmful species self-destructed toward extinction. Or at the very least unfollowed us on social media.

This Time of Trouble - this *Time of Trump* - relied on two types of humans to let it flourish; the above-noted *Homo Brutalis* - with their dogged pursuit of profit, power, and pain - and the comfortably complicit. They don't have a specific classification because they dwell on *Both Sides* of the issues. They are the Normalizers, Timid Institutionalists, Enablers, and Apologists. Those who keep the systemic cycle of dysfunction active generation after generation for various reasons, none of which benefits progess.

One day, future generations will look back on these so-called people with bemused confusion, cringe, and exclaim, "What a bunch of assholes!"

We in the present agree. Because we know them to be on the wrong side. The wrong side of the issues. The wrong side of the arguments. The wrong side of politics, culture, and society.

The Wrong Side of History!

> "In our world you were either a bully, a toady, or one of the nameless rabble of victims."
>
> -- Jean Shepherd, narrating as the adult Ralphie, in *A Christmas Story* (1983).

The Wrong Side of History's
DISCLAIMER

This book is not intended to educate, enlighten, inform, or to play well with others. It is a satirical compilation of caricatures based upon social media memes that publicly originated in late 2017 on the Twitter account @Marlowinc.

The subjects contained herein are mocked, parodied, and ridiculed with the presumption that those who read this book are aware of recent sociopolitical events leading up to the summer of 2020, and don't need much *hand-holding* with identifying people, places & events 'cuz they're smart & hip. Names have been changed/altered for legal reasons, but let's face it, these are public figures, the majority of which are deserving of the disrespectful treatment they receive.

The information written in this book - most of it taking on the form of outlined bullet points - was inspired by research, common knowledge, generally accepted public perception, and basic facts which are incredibly easy to search, find, and verify. Sources of all quotes, even the tweets, are properly cited.

There are over 200 caricatures throughout this book, that's barely scratching the surface with *The Wrong Side of History*'s never-ending membership. Chances are a few didn't make it, so please don't write in saying, "You forgot so-and-so," or "What about what's-their-name?" There are plenty enough of these deplorables, there just wasn't enough time. This book needed to get out before the 2020 election.

It is the goal of this book to combine satire, political/social humor, snarkiness, sarcasm, ad hominem, irony, bad puns, personal opinion, empirical knowledge, and bitter experience mixed in with the actual research. Some of the jok*e*s are a little blue, and others may make you see red.

A sense of humor is very important.

As far as *The Right Side of History* goes, best to avoid designating that title to anyone or anything in the present. That's a serious, dignified, and noble topic. This book is definitely *not* the format for it.

> "It never stops, and I wouldn't have it any other way. I try to learn from the past, but I plan for the future by focusing exclusively on the present. That's where the fun is. And if it can't be fun, what's the point?"
> -- *Trump: The Art of the Deal* by Donald J. Trump & Tony Schwartz, 1987.

¯_(ツ)_/¯

DONNY DOLL-HANDS

- A BIG menace with a tiny grasp of things.
- Rapist. Racist.
- Dictator fan boy.
- Forever impeached.
- Covfefe COVIDiot.
- Failure in:
  - Real estate.
  - Reality TV.
  - Actual reality.
- Con artist.
- Traitor. Russian puppet.
- Policy of Cruelty.
- Stochastic terrorist.
- Enemy of Democracy.
- Negligent genocide.

"Why can't we use nuclear weapons?"

-- Donald Trump asked a foreign policy expert advising him why the U.S. can't use nuclear weapons, MSNBC's Joe Scarborough said on the air, citing an unnamed source who claimed he had spoken with the GOP presidential nominee. August 2016

- *Favorite* Daughter.
- Shiksa Appeal.
- Handbag designer for the United Nations.
- Failed Daddy Wrangler.
- Best buds with Putin's gal pal.
- Suppressor of childhood memories.
- Brand name: *Complicit*.
- Unappreciated "Millennial."
- Conflict of interest: Made in China.
- Owns trademarks on voting machines.
- Champion of Working Moms With Nannies.
- Gets to sit in on ALL the meetings.

"I think it's the human condition to be frequently embarrassed by your parents."

-- Harper's Bazaar magazine September 2007

"PRINCESS"

KUSHY

"I know I've done good things, I know I've done bad things."

-- New York Magazine July 2009

- Son-In-Outlaw.
- A Jack-Of-No-Trades.
- Failed to disclose ...everything!
- Back-channel communicator.
- Slumlord.
- Overworked & Under-qualified.
- Broke the Middle East.
- Real estate father: Convicted criminal.
- Real estate father-in-law: Impeached criminal.
- Defender of Anti-Semites.
- Private email account to conduct WH business.
- Speaks only when unspoken.

- Formerly The "Smart" One.
- E-mails & DMs a specialty.
- Co-Trustee of a family "business" propped up with Russian rubles.
- *American Psycho.*
- White hunter. Black heart. Tiny penis.
- Amateur liar.
- A defense attorney's nightmare client.
- Subject of many Better Business Bureau complaints.
- Will probably indict himself.
- The douche doesn't fall far from the bag.
- That stupid "hobo beard."

"I'm kind of a closet redneck"

-- Interview on SiriusXM radio show *The Six Pack.* December 2017

DONNY DUMBASS, JR.

DOOFUS DRUMPF

"We have all the funding we need out of Russia."

-- Spoken to writer James Dodson in 2014 during a round of golf.

- "I'm ERIC!"
- Prone to acts of virulence.
- Charity case/front for daddy's love/payouts.
- The "Lenny" to his older brother's "George."
- Co-Trustee of a family business that can't be trusted.
- Proof that nepotism has its limits.
- Trust-fund toady.
- Favorite family traditions:
   -Sucking up to father figures.
   -Re-tweeting Nazis.
   -Looking stupid on TV.
- All that money & they still can't fix his damned teeth.

MELANOMA

- 'Murica's Third Lady.
- Be Best: Do as we say, ignore what we do.
- Seems to avoid coat sleeves.
- Joyless Christmas decorator inspired by *The Shining*.
- Has a particular "skill" with speech writing.
- Exists in a gilded purgatory reenforced by misery & greed.
- Quick with the hand slaps.
- A marriage built on:
  - A "me first" philosophy.
  - Birtherism.
  - Lies & infidelity.
  - Filthy lucre.
- REALLY doesn't care, do u?

"...I tell him my opinions, I tell him what I think. Sometimes he listens, sometimes he don't."

-- "Melania Trump: Donald and I Don't Always Agree" by Sarah Begley. *TIME Magazine*, February 24, 2016.

The Wrong Side of History's
FAMILY ALBUM

The *origins* of one's behavior obviously stems from *upbringing & influence*. Both *nature & nurture* are *crucial* factors. When those sources are a *contaminated* gene pool & a social circle of self-serving, greedy *malcontents*, the probability of a *deviant destiny* is rather *high*.

MEIN DRUMPF
- Patient zero of the Trump virus.
- An actual argument *against* immigrants & anchor babies.
- Was kicked out of Germany for being an asshole.
- The inspiration for his grandson's military service deferments.
- Pimp & privateer.
- Note to time travelers: Stop him from procreating.

ROY CRONY
- Self-loathing cocksucker who died in the darkest of closets.
- Joe McCarthy's attack poodle.
- The ethics & morals of a starving, rabid hyena.
- Mentor & legal consigliere to a young Donny Doll-Hands.
- Career boost from corpses of the Rosenbergs.
- Perjurer. Witness tamperer.
- Petty, vindictive creep.

DEAD FRED
- Real estate mogul, i.e. Slum lord golem.
- 1927's KKKing of Queens.
- Villain in a Woody Guthrie folk tune.
- Violator of the Fair Housing Act.
- Government contract conman.
- America, if not the world, was burdened with the vile legacy of such awful, cruel parenting skills.

MOMMY DREAREST
- The Ice Queen of the Damned.
- From whose womb the worst emerged.
- Hated being on the receiving end of her outsourced & failed maternal instincts.
- "What kind of son have I created?"
  --*Vanity Fair* 9/1/1990

PASTOR PENCE

- The Calm Liar.
- A Christian cypher.
- Sanctimonious fundamentalist.
- Self-loathing closet case enabling intolerance toward LGBTQ.
- Mommy issues.
- Anti-Science.
- Has faith that a pandemic can be prayed away.
- Probably believes *The Handmaid's Tale* is a how-to manual.
- Chuckly ass-kisser.
- Knows "nothing" about "anything" regarding Donny Doll-Hands, the one true love of his life.

"I fear Mrs. Pence more than I fear voters."

-- Pence, in 2007, on why he supported the annual automatic pay increase for members of Congress.

WILLY "LOW" BARR

- The Great "Summarizer."
- Trump's Human Cop Blocker.
- Defender of Republican criminals since the Reagan years.
- Go-to guy if you need a human right violated.
- Patronizing patriarchal vocal fry.
- Believes in the Rule of Law ...for controlling the powerless.
- Supplies the fuel that properly gaslights a nation.
- DOJ SOB = GOP SOP.
- Viral spreader of an Epstein-Barr style of justice.
- Another corrupt, aging white dude who fucks up America for his own personal privilege.

"...while this report does not conclude that the President committed a crime, it also does not exonerate him."

-- RE: Special Counsel Robert Mueller's Russia Investigation.

March 24 2019

MR. POMPOUS

- Secretary of Misstates.
- No idea that actions/words have consequences.
- Bellicose rhetoric a specialty
- Needs help finding Ukraine on a map.
- Directed the CIA ...away from its patriotic duties.
- Contradicts himself to the point of non-existence.
- Spotlight grabber.
- Torture-defending Islamophobe.
- Reckless diplomacy.
- Kochsucker who hates the gays.

"I eat and breathe small government and freedom."

-- From the article "An Officer And A Free Marketeer," July 29, 2011. Published in the conservative newspaper *Human Events*.

- Hedge Funder. '80s movie villain.
- Slayer of widows & orphans.
- King of the Foreclosures.
- Confuses cutting with growth.
- Hollywood Producer: *Rules Don't Apply*.
- Married to a "Marie Antoinette" dominatrix.
- Ethics violator.
- Tax money abuser.
- Manure recipient.
- Confuses profit with human emotions.
- Justification for proletarian revolutions.

"I have very good friends on Wall Street."

-- May 9th, 2016 *NY Times* article: "Donald Trump's Pick for Fund-Raiser Is Rife With Contradictions."

THE MUNCHER
"WRINKLES" ROSS

"My wife... sometimes accuses me of trying to reinvent the 19th century. In some ways she's right because I like things that I can understand and that aren't too complicated."

-- From an interview on CNBC's "I Am American Business," Nov. 30, 2012.

- Big fan of:
  - Commerce.
  - Bankruptcy.
  - Dilapidated structures.
- Business ties to Russian oligarchs.
- Launders his money & his adult diapers separately.
- Another rich d-bag who "forgets" to disclose things during confirmation processes.
- Lies about personal wealth to impress other rich d-bags.
- Thinks a pandemic is good for business.
- Calcium deprived.

1%

MICK MALEVOLENCE

- Baby-faced Gríma Wormtongue.
- Chief demonizer of America's poor.
- Bad acting in the White House.
- Obsequious little runt.
- Tea Party toady.
- 1% Pamperer.
- Protects Corporations from annoying Consumers.
- Staunch critic of the Bureau he pretended to head.
- The Bizarro Elizabeth Warren.
- Supports cuts to humanitarian programs.
- Dickensian little shit.

"I don't like the fact that C.F.P.B. exists, I will be perfectly honest with you."

-- Stated during a House Congressional subcommittee hearing on the Consumer Financial Protection Bureau, June 25, 2015.

- Amway Ponzi Schemer.
- Proof that Wealthy ≠ Educated.
- Student loans = Indentured servitude.
- Brother's a big Hermann Göring fan.
- Pay-for-Play.
- Educational policies:
  Proselytize for profit!
  Guns against grizzly bears!
  The 1% > Public schools.
- Aliases:
  - B. DeValued.
  - Cruella DeVoucher.
  - Helena Bent-on Charters.
- A dangerous dunce in need of detention.

"There is nothing in the data that would suggest that kids being back in school is dangerous to them."

-- Said during a pandemic by someone who has no skin in the game, but lots to financially gain. CNN's *State of the Union*. July 12, 2020.

BETSY DeVOID

AGITA PAI

"The Internet has enriched my own life immeasurably."

-- During a FCC hearing for the repeal of Net Neutrality rules. December 14, 2017

- Corporate shill. ISP whore.
- Murderer of Net Neutrality.
- A major FCCer.
- That stupid, oversized coffee mug.
- A punchable face.
- Guilty of fraud & ethics violations.
- Associates with right-wing conspirators.
- Director of the worst internet videos.
- Smug mocker.
- Yarp.

KELLYANNE CONJOB

- Political mercenary.
- Bowling Green Massacre survivor.
- The Mouth of Sauron in a blonde fright wig.
- Failed comedian.
- Alternative facts.
- Apologist & rationalist of horrific, monstrous things!
- Claims microwave ovens are spying on her.
- When she lies, Democracy dies.
- Camera hog.
- Violator of the truth & the Hatch Act.
- Hell's Perky Cheerleader.

"I never knew how ugly and how stupid I was until, you know, we had Twitter."

-- During a guest appearance on the talk show *The View*, September 2016

"KILLER" MILLER

- High School Yearbook: Most likely to be a fascist, elitist twat.
- Lied about his grandmother's death from COVID-19. Scorned by his family.
- Adviser & speechwriter for the dementedly privileged.
- Despised by janitors everywhere.
- A walking R-Complex.
- BFF to Neo-Nazis.
- The Statue of Liberty's Arch-Enemy.
- Brainiac behind the travel bans.
- Renfield for the Right-wing.
- Delights in child snatching & family separations.
- In the "Extremists Files" of the Southern Poverty Law Center.
- "He's Waffen-SS"

"I think to say that 'We're in control' would be a substantial understatement."

-- Response during an interview on CBS news program *Face The Nation* February 12, 2017.

HERR GÖRK

"It's this constant, 'Oh, it's the white man. It's the white supremacists. That's the problem.' No, it isn't..."

-- *Breitbart News Daily* radio show. Days before the August 2017 rally in Charlottesville, VA where white supremacists were the problem.

- Former WH National Security Aide. Ongoing Nationalist.
- Collector of concealed weapons & funny fascist medals.
- Misinterprets quotes from Holocaust survivors.
- Banned from YouTube.
- Stupidly attacks his betters, such as journalist Brian Karem.
- Anti-Muslim. Anti-Semitic. Anti-Human.
- Creepy ideologue. Creepier accent.
- Fake PhD.
- Toxic alpha male wannabe.
- A very bad apologist.
- Thinks he's hot snot on a silver platter, but he's just a cold booger on a paper plate.

- Prominent gas giant.
- Plotted against US sanctions to profit from Siberian oil deal.
- A fool for fossil fuel.
- Russian "Order of Friendship" medal winner.
- Interactive Putin ally.
- Viewed the State Department as a freelance gig.
- Worked for a "fucking moron."
- Desperately trying to deny all of the above.

"My philosophy is to make money."

-- March 7, 2013 interview on *CBS This Morning*.

REXXON

GENERAL KILLJOY

"He's gone off the rails. We're in Crazytown."

-- About Donald Trump. From Bob Woodward's book *Fear: Trump in the White House*.

- Failed at being the adult in a room.
- Patronizing Patriarch.
- Ego fluffed a Criminal Narcissist.
- Sacrificed integrity of career, dead son to ensure a lousy government pension.
- Respects women ...in an objectifying, 1950s, anti-feminist sort of way.
- US Civil War bothsiderist.
- Easily "stunned" by critics.
- Typical hard-right jerk.
- Profits from the private prison industry.
- Served in a war in which his former boss received 5 deferments.

CAP'N KOOK

- War monger and mustache enthusiast.
- Arch-enemy of the United Nations.
- People skills of a feral wolverine.
- Book sales before country.
- Replies to minor conflicts with nuclear threats & throwing office supplies.
- Employed by two of the worst WH Administrations.
- Regime Change Chimera.
- Booster of failed neoconservative policies.
- Iraq War Cheerleader.
- Iran-Contra Cover-Upper.
- The Anti-diplomat.
- One Crazy Asshole.

"I am not a professional politician."

-- From a *National Review* article "Bolton for President: A 'Goldwater Conservative'," Oct. 1, 2010.

LOOSE BANNON

- Breitbart Pretty Boy.
- Human cold sore.
- Professional paranoid.
- Cambridge Analytica liaison.
- Champion for the Wrong Side of History.
- Mercer whore.
- Walking barf bag.
- Domestic abuser.
- Faux Outsider.
- *We Build The Wall* was really *We Bilk Them All*.
- Proof that White Supremacy is a recessive trait.
- Accused of self-fellatio. *Okaaay....*

"Darkness is good. Dick Cheney. Darth Vader. Satan. That's power."

-- From a Nov. 18, 2016 article in *The Hollywood Reporter*.

FLYNTY

"I've been called an extremist."

-- Trying to justify the phrase "radical Islam" during a July 2016 Heritage Foundation event.

- Also known as "Flipper."
- General nuisance.
- Doesn't play well with others.
- Tried to kidnap a fugitive cleric for a bit of Turkish delight.
- Big fan of Russian Television Network.
- Lock ~~her~~ *him* up!
- Sanctions, schmanctions!
- Susceptible to blackmail.
- Named names to protect his d-bag son.
- Plead guilty despite a corrupt DOJ.

SHORT SESSIONS

- Master Recuser.
- Believes in the American Justice System ...circa 18th century.
- Hobbies:
  - Zealotry.
  - Lying.
  - Racism.
  - Height envy.
- DOJ accomplishments:
  - Threatened sanctuary cities.
  - *Reefer Madness* inspired drug policy.
  - Cherry-picked Bible passages to justify human rights violations.
- Lawful Evil Halfling.

"Republicans do not believe in identity politics."

-- During an interview on Fox News, June 7, 2009.

KURSED JEN

"We do not have any intention right now to shoot at people."

-- Referring to US troops deployed to the southern border as incoming migrants sought asylum. October 25, 2018.

- Former Secretary of the DHS: Child Catcher Division.
- Persona non grata at Mexican restaurants.
- Supervised Trumps's immigration policy *Kages4Kids*.
- Participant in the slow, disastrous 2005 Hurricane Katrina response.
- Doubles down on the arrogance when called out by the press.
- Ironically ruins professional rep while beefing up résumé.
- A career technocrat incapable of expressing human empathy.

- Another Trump flunky who wanted to destroy the department he led.
- That asshole who laughs at his own offensive jokes.
- Under SO MANY investigations.
- Climate-denying clodhopper.
- Putin fan boy.
- Every *Captain Planet* villain rolled into one.
- Pimped out National Parks to deregulated industries.
- Bully. Thug. Criminal. Racist. That's just his résumé info.
- Made Scott Pollutit look like the Lorax.

"The climate is changing; I don't think you can deny that. But climate has always changed."

-- Being his usual fuckwad self in an *L.A. Times* interview. Dec. 15, 2016.

ZTINKY

SCOTT POLLUTIT

"Threats I have faced are unprecedented."

-- Persecution complex on full display during a *CBS News* interview. February 28, 2018.

- Climate change denier & EPA rapist.
- Paranoid obsessed with security.
- High maintenance luxury whore.
- Reversed environmental policies as part of a spite & greed agenda.
- Shady housing arrangements.
- The Very Expensive Phone Booth.
- Chick-Fil-A feather plucker.
- The "Used Hotel Mattress" King.
- Ritz-Carlton lotion tester.
- Forced to quit EPA as a momentary media deflection from the crimes of his boss.

HUCKLEBERRY

- Smokey-Eyed Fake News Fomenter.
- Dad eats squirrels & tells very bad jokes.
- Brother has "particular rapport" with dogs.
- Aided, abetted & enabled Worst. Administration. *EVER*.
- Enemy of the 1st Amendment.
- Drawls own conclusions.
- Discredits journalists.
- Uses own kids as human shields from criticism.
- Uses God as an all-purpose shield from truth.

"Just because reporters say something over and over and over again doesn't start to make it true."

-- During an appearance on ABC's *This Week* February 26, 2017.

BABY SPICER

"The President and a small group of people know exactly what he meant."

-- Regarding "covfefe" at a May 2017 White House press briefing.

- Former Press Secretary of Gaslighting.
- The Keeper of Notes.
- Lousy liar sadly seeking redemption.
- Ex-Easter Bunny for Bush in 2008.
- Hid in the White House bushes to cowardly avoid the press.
- Turn-offs:
  - Q & A sessions
  - Melissa McCarthy movies.
  - Russian salad dressing.
  - Pushing his lousy book.
  - Dippin' Dots
- Right-winger with two left feet.
- Will gladly share his passwords.

The Wrong Side of History's
EXECUTIVE DYSFUNCTION

Being part of *America's Crime Syndicate* is not an easy job. Oh sure, there are the perks of profitable kickbacks, settling old scores, and undermining Democracy, but there's also a *massive ego* that needs to be fed, stroked & called *pretty* in front of news cameras.

The following are a select assortment of **corrupt minions** who had to keep their boss *happy* as they contaminated & befouled the *executive branch* of the United States Government.

ELAINE CHINTZ
- Secretary of Questionable Imports/Exports.
- Having a shady family business qualified her to work for Trump.
- Carved out a special path for "Kentucky Only" projects.
- Oversees all the slow boats to China.
- She can't get enough of tiny turtle tadger.

AMBIEN CARSON
- Proof you don't have to be a brain surgeon to be a brain surgeon.
- Blamed wife on picking out his $31K tax-payer funded dining room furniture.
- Man of ~~science~~ magical thinking.
- HUD dud whose in way over his sleepy, little head.

SCHTICK PERRY
- Wanted to eliminate, but forgot the name of, the Dept. he ended up heading.
- "Christian" with no values.
- *The 3 Amigos: Ukraine-Style!*
- Another Texan with an insatiable bloodlust & low intellect.
- Pseudoscientist in charge of nuclear weapons.
- Had more dignity on *Dancing With The Stars*.

LUSHY KUDLOW
- National Economic Council Director & Mixologist.
- Thinks anyone who interviews him is named "Chucktodd."
- Trump Tax Cut Defender.
- The Criswell of economic & financial predictions.
- Sees Greenland as an impulse buy.
- It's 4pm somewhere in the world marketplace.

The Wrong Side of History's
EXECUTIVE DYSFUNCTION

@RealDonaldTrump
September 26, 2019:
THE GREATEST SCAM IN THE HISTORY OF AMERICAN POLITICS!

STEPHIE GRIMACE ★ ★ ★
- Surpassed her Press Secretary predecessors by avoiding the legitimate press altogether.
- Her publicly funded office ensured Trumps' ass was kissed & the Hatch Act was violated.
- 1st Amendment antagonist.
- Fired from past jobs due to cheating & plagiarism.
- AZ State Trooper nickname: *Speedy Gonz-oholic*.

WINCE PROBUS ★ ★ ★
- As with his party, he swallowed his principals in the name of power.
- Former WH Chief of Staff & Oval Office Gimp.
- Fascist appeaser.
- Played the part of the nervous courtier to a mad & spiteful king.
- Fired by tweet.
- Re-hired to a lesser position.

MATT WIDELOAD ★ ★ ★

- The Missing Link between Sessions & Barr.
- Cast to act as the DOJ's AG by a Reality Show POTUS.
- Puts the "Ox" in "Lummox."
- Used the legal system as a political weapon for profit.
- Gets sweaty & belligerent when questioned.
- Has a biblical view of justice.

FINICKY NIKKI ★ ★ ★

- Principles shift depending on which way the Confederate flag blows.
- Trump's former U.N. enforcement flunky.
- Adopts a See No Evil approach to her political decisions.
- A "Do as we say, NOT as we do" approach to international human rights.

The Wrong Side of History's
EXECUTIVE DYSFUNCTION

@RealDonaldTrump
February 18, 2017:
Don't believe the main stream (fake news) media. The White House is running VERY WELL. I inherited a MESS and am in the process of fixing it.

HOPE HEXED ★★★★
- The Communications Director who didn't give interviews.
- POTUS pants blow-dryer.
- Turn-ons: Dumb, abusive married men.
- Turn-offs: Investigative spotlights.
- Hired as administrative eye candy.
- Trump's mean girl ghost-tweeter.

SPAM CLOVERS ★★★★
- Recruiter & vetter of Carter "Cagey" Page.
- Part of the Papadop/Russia email circle jerk.
- A decaying bag of beef rejected by the USDA.
- Tea Party activist.
- Harry Potter's muggle uncle with a MAGA hard-on.
- Fled at the first hint of trouble.

TOM INHUMAN ★★★★
- The ICE man cometh & goeth.
- Enemy of sanctuary cities.
- Just another cruel thug who vilified "Illegal immigrants" to justify racist policies.
- A true Deplorable.
- Rationalizes detention centers via bad faith & bellowing like a silverback ape.

MOOCHY ★★★★
- Former White House Director of Bada Bing!
- Went from Trump's Top Trash Talker to Persona Non *Grazie* in ten days.
- Foul-mouthed dandy.
- Burns bridges before crossing them.
- Abandoned pregnant wife for cheap career boost.

RUDY GALOONY

- Speech pattern: A noun, a verb, and 9/11.
- Screechy, authoritarian race-baiter.
- 'Murica's Mayor.
- Fraud Guarantee! Mafia Rave!
- Political sycophant.
  Social psychopath.
- Law & order = Stop & frisk.
- Always defending the wrong side of whatever side there is.
- Wall Street ~~enemy~~ sweetheart.
- Thin-skinned. Thick-witted.
- Champion of cronyism.
- Vindictive bully.
- Giggling blabbermouth.
- Putin praiser.

"It's about time law enforcement got as organized as organized crime."

-- *"The Sicilian Connection"* by Peter Stoler.
TIME Magazine, October 15, 1984.

CODGER STAIN

- Lifetime Ratfucker.
- Has a Dick pic on his back.
- WikiLeaks colluder.
- Sexist. Racist. Malignant cyst.
- Gollum stand-in.
- Opportunistic traitor.
- Traitorous opportunist.
- Microcephalic sociopath.
- Discredited researcher.
- Failed cosplayer.
- Untrustworthy even by right-wing standards.
- Unpardonable sinner.
- A sentence commuted doesn't imply innocence.

"I am so ready. Let's get it on. Prepare to die cocksucker."

-- Part of a threatening April 9, 2018 email sent to stand-up comic, and grand jury witness, Randy Credico.
Breaking the law is just second nature to this abominable homunculus.

THE MAN FORT

- Influence peddler.
- Dictator groupie.
- No moral or legal compass.
- Ukraine-ophile.
- Money launderer.
- Extravagant clotheshorse.
- Russian ghostwriter.
- Bail welcher.
- Plea deal promise breaker.
- Collector of ankle bracelet monitors.
- $15K ostrich jacket.
- Just couldn't stop doin' bad things.

"I'm always careful what clients I take."

-- In response to Chuck Todd's softball question "And are you going to make a promise in the future that if he's president, you'll be careful what clients you take?" *Meet The Press*, April 10, 2016.

- High Level Coffee Boy /Low Level Entry-Point.
- Conservative think tank intern.
- How To Succeed In Treason Without Really Trying.
- Too many Cyrillic letters in his email contact list.
- "Plea-deal-opoulos."
- Became famous in a not-good way.
- Prison sentence wasn't long enough.

"Russia has been eager to meet with Mr. Trump for some time and have been reaching out to me to discuss."

-- In an email sent to Paul Manafort. May 4, 2016.

PAPADOP

CARTER CAGEY

"The dark cloud was darkest over myself."

-- While testifying before Congress' Permanent Select Committee on Intelligence. Nov. 2, 2017.

- Foreign-policy adviser for Trump's 2016 Presidential campaign ...until suddenly he wasn't.
- Favorite bumper sticker: "I ♥ Moscow!"
- Highly regarded as being totally forgettable.
- Self-incriminating bull-shitter.
- Is only walking around free due to legal technicalities & FBI sloppiness.
- Poker tell: Very giggly when lying.
- Accidentally corroborated Steele Dossier.
- Kremlin ass-kisser.
- Suspicious activities & weird hats.

- Manhandler. Woman assaulter.
- Pundit Thug.
- Abused access to White House as a faux lobbyist.
- Belligerent Defender of the Dumb.
- Failed campaign manager.
- Motto: Let Trump be Trump.
- Equally hated on both sides of the political spectrum.
- Expresses himself via public, unhinged rants.
- #WompWomp
- Goon.

"Everything is politically correct nowadays."

-- His response on *Hannity* to the charge of battery against him for grabbing & bruising a *Breitbart News* reporter. April 14, 2016.

SCREW N. DOWSKI

BRAD PROSKULL

"I do not have any firsthand knowledge of foreign interference in the 2016 election."

-- Very careful wording from a November 3, 2017 letter to top Democrats on the House Judiciary and Oversight committees.

- Over-promoted IT troll & merch hawker.
- Cambridge Analytica interlocutor.
- Trump's online enabler.
- MAGA rally production costs include legal fees to cover music rights violations.
- Hacked 2020 campaign with updated 2016 malware.
- A toxic nerd spreading social media diseases.
- "Death Star" destroyed by a Resistance force of TikTok teens & K-pop stans.
- Grifting & scamming all the way to Election Day.
- WTF is up with his weird head?

The Wrong Side of History's
CAMPAIGN CLEAN-UP

The 2016 Presidential race left a long, *lingering* scar on the American psyche. Many factors were in play as determined, *hostile forces* sewed chaos & doubt among the electorate. The dubious results violated the *Will of The People* and ignored the *popular vote*.

The following is a collection of conspiratorial confetti, deplorable bunting, and other felonious flotsam & jetsam found scattered about on a cluttered arena floor one harsh, cold November morning.

MIKEY "FIX-IT"
- From Trump's Special Counsel to Congress' Special Witness.
- Tom Hagen wannabe.
- The mobbed-up missing link between scandal & treason.
- "Stormy" problems a specialty.
- Sean Hannity's Pro Bono.
- Business expense: Mistress pay-offs.
- "Says who?"

JUNIOR FLYNTY
- Intel Group chief of staff, top aide, & reason for his dad's flipping.
- Hubris on overload.
- Chip off the Ol' Blockhead.
- Ran *Pizzagate* delivery.
- Victimhood claimant.
- Over-privileged Dude-Bro.
- Oaf. Goon.

BORIS ASININE
- Eric Trump's college buddy & 2016 campaign surrogate.
- Sinclair Broadcast stooge.
- Very, *very* brief WH spokesman.
- His Must-run segments were a mostly-miss must-avoid.
- Anger management failure.
- Yes, he's as stupid & mean as he looks.

RICK GALOOT
- Client short list:
  -- Ukrainian President.
  -- Russian oligarchs.
- Manafort's ex-partner in crime.
- Money launderer, perjurer, fraudster & embezzler.
- Took the fall for Melania's speech plagiarism.
- Conspired against his own country.

GREED OVER PEOPLE

- Thoughts & prayers & empty promises.
- Election cheaters. Political whores.
- Racists. Misogynists. Homophobes. Xenophobes. Transphobes. All-around Assholes.
- Faux Christians. Pseudo Patriots.
- No to: Science. Education. The Environment. Democracy. Civilization.
- Party over Country.
- Propaganda over Truth.
- Pro-Life until you're post-natal.
- Hate the poor & sick.
- Agenda: Turn America into a medieval feudal system with them as divine royalty.
- Dinosaurs doing damage as they die off.

"Every time we sing, *God Bless America*, we are asking for help."

--- From the last paragraph of the GOP.com Preamble.

SENATOR YERTLE

- Defender of perverts, crooks, & traitors with a (R) next to their names.
- Held SCOTUS seat hostage for a year.
- Makes up the rules as he goes.
- Recedes into shell when Persistent Women are nearby.
- Pimped out the US to Russia for political vanity projects.
- Considers it rude to impeach wife's boss.
- Slow & steady steals the Senate vote.
- #MoscowMitch

"We need to be honest with the public."

-- From an Oct. 23, 2010, Q&A interview with the *National Journal* regarding the mid-term election and his failed scheme to make Barack Obama a one-term president.

LINDZEE!

- Senator Grandstand.
- Booster of Brett "Boof" Kavanaugh.
- Potty mouthed pontificator.
- Pro-life war hawk.
- Pearl-clutching drama queen.
- Tossed his spine into McCain's coffin.
- Self-loathing closet case.
- Pusher of debunked Benghazi-isms.
- Trump apparatchik.
- Career opportunist.
- Dedicated misogynist.
- Kompromat is a helluva drug!

"It's one thing to shoot yourself in the foot. Just don't reload the gun."

-- Spoken during a November 2012 interview on CBS' *Face The Nation*, concerning the topics of immigration reform, the GOP losing the Hispanic vote, & other issues he used to care about.

- Eye "doctor" suffering from cultural myopia and social astigmatism.
- Anti-vax & other debunked conspiracy theories.
- Ayn Rand fanboy.
- Benghazi investigation point man.
- Provokes ill-tempered neighbors via acts of passive-aggressive lawn maintenance.
- Mealy apple that didn't fall far from the rotted tree.
- Coal industry check depositor.
- Trump's errand boy for Russia.
- Paleolibertarian in a fright wig.

"We live in a democracy, and people are free to sometimes choose the wrong leader."

-- An obfuscated response to a question on NPR regarding President Obama's SOTU speech. Feb. 14, 2013.

RANDOM PALL

TEDDY CRUISER

"Nobody cares what any politician in Washington says."

-- Meaningless platitude tossed out at a so-called Republican Leadership Conference. June 2014.

- Fatuous Self-Aggrandizer.
- Misinterprets Dr. Seuss stories & *The Simpsons* to push right-wing propaganda/agenda.
- Healthcare Hypocrite.
- Will sell out father, wife, self-dignity for ephemeral political approval.
- Oily man with an abrasive rep.
- Theocrat who gets booed by fellow fundamentalists.
- College classmates recall him as the Cruisin' Creep.
- The senator that other senators love to hate.
- Embraced Zodiac Killer joke to deflect from his own awfulness.

- Rule of law hypocrite.
- Placed a strangling Koch hold on the EPA.
- A legislative terrorist, according to former House Speaker John Boehner.
- A pathological aversion to suit jackets.
- Favorite wrestling moves at OSU:
  - The memory lock.
  - The clean & jerk cover up.
  - The vindication grasp & clutch.
- Undermines House Oversight.
- Trump's personal athletic cup.
- Goes to the mat defending molesters.
- Constantly body-slammed by facts & public shaming.

"I think there are a number of us who are going to push back on that real, real hard."

-- Fake tough-guy rhetoric covering up his crybaby reaction in having to follow bipartisan House Committee rules. Oct. 19, 2018.

JUNGLE GYM JORDAN

MATT PUTZ

"For the good of the American people, we must place our own interests first."

-- From his ass-kissing op-ed in the S. Florida *SunSentinel* "President Trump proves America is his top priority" April 28, 2017.

- "Florida Man" fighting the "Deep State."
- Freedom Caucus punchline.
- Smug mansplaining Trumpanzee.
- NRA Rating: A+. Humanities: F.
- Stands his ground against breathalyzers.
- Believes humans aren't affecting the climate as he plots the EPA's destruction.
- Opposes sanctuary cities.
- Asked a right-wing Holocaust denier to be his State of The Union date.
- Law-breaking goon squad leader.
- Hoarder of speeding tickets.
- Testy witness tamperer.

- Congressman. Empty suit.
- Trump Transition Team member.
- Failed farmer.
- White House lurker & errand boy.
- Russia "Investigator."
- Twitter avatar provocateur.
- Distractor. Obstructor.
- Failed recuser.
- Master of the frivolous lawsuit.
- House Intelligence Committee's self-designated "lone wolf."
- Uber's fav customer.
- Hates that confirmed Steele Dossier.
- Re: Memo.

"It's important to be honest and truthful with your constituents. At the end of the day, we represent them."

-- He was complaining about the "lemmings" attitude of his fellow GOP. From a *National Review* article, "Devin Nunes, Provocateur", Oct. 7, 2013.

DEVIN MOO-NES

GOOMER!

"You spend a couple million dollars running for Congress, people get tired of seeing your face."

-- Speech at the David Horowitz Freedom Center's Texas Weekend. May 3, 2013

- GOP Congressman from Texas (Insert punchline here).
- Another pro-lifer who undermines support for the postnatal.
- A black hole of pure stupidity.
- Tea Party Birtherist (i.e. Racist twerp).
- Shames shooting victims for not shooting back.
- Do not cast aspersions on his asparagus.
- Argues Hilary conspired with Russia in 2016 election.
- Wets himself over "terror babies."
- Jesus hates taxes!
- Madman off his meds.
- Blamed his face mask for catching COVID.

- Poster boy for white male mediocrity.
- Political credo: Prefers to die on the stupidest of hills.
- Parenthood should not be Planned.
- The most Minor of Leaders.
- Trump's toadying taint licker.
- Pearl-clutching public diatribes.
- Blames social media filters & search engine algorithms for doing their jobs.
- Took "donations" in:
  - Ukrainian hyrvnias.
  - Saudi riyals.
- Public lands are just asking for it.
- An empty suit filled with archaic, Republican rhetoric.

"There's...there's two people, I think, Putin pays: Rohrabacher and Trump... [laughter]...swear to God."

-- During a July 2016 conversation with fellow members of House leadership. In May 2017 McCarthy tweeted: "This was an attempt at humor gone wrong." Yeah, right.

CAVE-IN McCARTHY

JUDGE KALENDAR

"If the president does something dastardly, the impeachment process is available."

-- From "Separation of Powers During the Forty-Fourth Presidency and Beyond." A 2009 article "Bart" wrote for the *Minnesota Law Review*.

- Trump's Human Pardon.
- Won't shake hands but will cover mouths.
- The Forrest Gump of GOP politics.
- The Keeper of Bush/Cheney Secrets.
- Has the ethics of an '80s teen movie.
- Whatever it is, he's against it:
  - A woman's right to choose.
  - Net neutrality.
  - Gun control.
  - The environment.
  - Voting rights.
  - Consumer rights.
  - Human rights.
- Believes only a Democratic POTUS is indictable.
- Practiced as a ~~lawyer~~ liar.
- The angriest boofer.

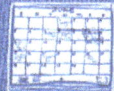

The Wrong Side of History's
PARTISAN POLITICS

When in the course of *inhuman events*, one political party deems it *"necessary"* to dissolve impartiality, fairness, progress, & a *functioning government* for the sake of *personally profiting* from the aforementioned inhuman events, to presume they have powers *over* the earth, and to allow their *ignorant opinions* to override truths self-evidently held, then it is up to *We The People* to alter or to *abolish* that political party.

Presented here are a quisling quorum of the U.S. Senators & Representatives who *no longer* respect the rule of law, who *ignore* the wishes of their **constituents**, and are just in it for themselves, draining resources on a global scale.

SUZIE SELL-OUT
- Reprimands via concerned finger waggings.
- Ethical cocktease.
- Leadership style of feckless ambiguity.
- Booster of Republican rapists.
- She'll have what McConnell is having.
- Her moral rationalizing foiled by Mitt Romney. Curses!

STEVE SCABIES
- Continued to advocate homophobia after a gay woman saved his life.
- *NO* lessons learned after being shot.
- Tea Party pipsqueak.
- Perpetual Dude-Bro.
- Predictable GOP team player.
- Election strategy: "I'm not a racist, but..."

ICK SCOTT
- The Creature From The Florida Swamps.
- A medical vampire whose track record includes:
  - Medicare fraud.
  - Drug testing kickbacks.
  - Pharmaceutical fraud.
  - Healthcare fear tactics.
- Destroyer of family planning services & clinics.
- Climate change denying bully.

LESSER CHENEY
- Daddy's Little Deferment.
- Carpetbagger.
- She's got her father's sneer & his lack of a heart.
- Sacrificed her sister for failed political gain.
- Pro-war. Pro-torture.
- POTUS power enabler. (GOP only).
- Sith apprentice bucking for that Darth title.

The Wrong Side of History's
PARTISAN POLITICS

@RealDonaldTrump
August 3, 2011:
Republicans gave Obama a free pass to the White House -- they just don't get it

DOUG HOLLERIN'
- Rebel yelling rube.
- Death penalty supporting theologian.
- Took a Koch pledge to vote against any Global Warming legislation.
- Tax cuts only for the rich.
- Belligerent blowhard & rapid ranter.
- Proves men are too shrill for politics.

FONI EARNEST
- Bread bags on her shoes.
- Planned Parenthood castigator & castrator.
- Betsy DeVos vetter.
- Plays fast & loose 'tween facts & opinions.
- Another politician who has no idea how government functions.
- Standard Tea Partier, opposed to all things progressive.

MARSHY BACKWOODS
- Bumpkin spice.
- Taylor Swift knew she was trouble ...trouble ...trouble.
- Violator of impeachment trial rules.
- Net Neutrality opposer.
- Science denier.
- Screw women's rights 'cuz she's got hers.
- So desperate to get Trump's attention.

STEVE KKKING
- Confederacy fan boy.
- Supporter of racial profiling policies.
- White genocide conspiracy theorist.
- Defines human ancestry as "rape & incest."
- All in for a total abortion ban.
- Sued by mom of "Success Kid" internet meme.

The Wrong Side of History's
PARTISAN POLITICS

@RealDonaldTrump
January 2, 2013:
This is a terrible deal for the country and an embarrassment for Republicans!

MAWKISH MEADOWS

- House Freedom Caucus-sucker.
- Red-meat Republi-can't.
- Ship-jumping rat.
- Trump butt-smoocher.
- Just another southern racist suffering from "white savior" syndrome.
- Thinks "truth" & "opinion" are the same.
- Idiot.

TOMMY ROTTEN

- Fear-mongering conspiracy theorist.
- Iran's unwanted pen pal.
- Leader of the #47Traitors.
- Torture enthusiast.
- "Bombing makes us safer."
- Believes food is too good for the poor.
- Know-nothing blowhard.
- Arrogant bully in need of a serious ass kicking.

MARCO THE RUBE

- Florida invertebrate.
- NRA's pocket lint.
- Replies to questions via a fish-flopping style.
- Failed GOP golden child.
- Dry mouth pontificator.
- Thoughtless prayers & empty Biblical tweets.
- From Never Trumper to MAGA door mat.

CHUCK CRABGRASS

- Patronizing midwesterner.
- Buzzkill to progress.
- A valid argument for term limits.
- A political voting record that reveals a miserable, partisan hack.
- Pushed thru all the wrong judges.
- Senile, old fart who thinks his shit doesn't stink.

The Wrong Side of History's
RUSSIAN GANG OF 8

July 4th, 2018: A group of Republican lawmakers ran off to Moscow to meet with Russian officials on Independence Day for no urgent reason other than to seek "a better relationship."

An unnecessary trip to conduct single-party negotiations, in secret, with such Putin flunkies as Russian Foreign Minister Sergey "Soviet Relic" Lavrov. The meetings were miserable failures.

Since they were representing Donny Doll-Hands & other GOP criminals, the Traitorous Eight were in *way* over their heads. The Russians whipped the Republican rubes like the greedy curs they were. A Duma lawmaker later said "this was one of the easiest" sit-downs he ever had with American officials.

FYI: Most of these politicians were known to disagree with various Trump White House policies prior to their Moscow visit. Afterwards ...well ...it's like they drank the vodka-flavored Kool-Aid.

WASHINGTON D.C.'S LEAST WANTED

KAY "THE LONE" GRANGER
Texas Representative
The token woman.

JOHN "EVEN STEVEN" HOEVEN
N. Dakota Senator
Mediocre centrist.

JOHN "NOT A REAL" KENNEDY
Louisiana Senator
Faux Good Ol' Boy.

RON "THE CON" JOHNSON
Wisconsin Senator
Dickish Tea Bagger.

JERRY "GET A BRAIN" MORAN
Kansas Senator
The Cowardly Liar.

RICHARD "POLITICAL WINDSOCK" SHELBY
Alabama Senator
Middling careerist.

STEVE "NO NICKNAME" DAINES
Montana Senator
He came. He saw. He concurred.

JOHN "STAY SAFE, GET SMALL" THUNE
S. Dakota Senator
A dystopia will have to do.

- Loser ex-congressman
- Putin's favorite drunken arm wrestler.
- Spent seven years shoving words in Ronald Reagan's pie-hole.
- Undermined the Magnitsky Act.
- WikiLeaks apologist.
- Political gaslighter.
- Rationalizes Russian policy with a Whataboutist perspective.
- Climate change denier.
- Proud defender of bad, awful & terrible folks.

"...Unless we provide consequences for activities and actions that are wrong, we are not going to get any truth."

-- Dana's opinion that he preferred to extort the U.N. rather than have the U.S. pay a fair share of important funding. June 17, 2005

DANA RUSSIABACKER

TREY GEEKY

"I'm unelectable in the District of Columbia."

-- From a July 6, 2011 article in *The New Republic*: "Meet Trey Gowdy, Tea Party Politician and D.C.'s Most Unlikely Friend."

- Was the moistest of legislators.
- Tea Party pencil-neck.
- Benghazi there, done that.
- Pro-life's Draco Malfoy.
- Bridge-burning concern troll.
- Pointed out problems while lacking solutions.
- A failure even by corrupt politician standards.
- Wasted money on investigations and barbers.
- Quit due to "incivility." ¯_(ツ)_/¯
- Wants to be a lobbyist when he grows up.
- Faux outrage partisan hack.
- Regrets? He's had a ~~few~~ lot.

- Doctor pandering to anti-vaxxers.
- Green Party Grifter.
- Recount Scammer.
- Purity Test Cheat.
- Darling of RTV Network.
- Putin's Useful Dupe.
- Proving the Left has its morons.
- Highest office held: Small Town Meeting Rep.
- Fur wearing faux hippie.
- WikiLeaks groupie.
- Electoral opportunist/bridesmaid.

"Hillary has the potential to do a whole lot more damage ...much more easily than Donald Trump could do his."

-- Demonstrating her political naiveté during a Sept. 2016 interview on POLITICO's *Off Message* podcast.

SHILL STEIN

TULSKI GRABBAG

"Ultimately, whether people like it or not, there are consequences to elections..."

-- During an interview on FOX's *Cavuto Live* she gleefully supported Trump's vengeful firing of Lt. Col. Vindman. Feb. 8, 2020.

- Electoral chaos agent who feeds on doubt.
- Lots of online supporters with Cyrillic letters in their posts.
- Mixed messages on:
  - progressive social issues.
  - abortion.
  - LGBTQ rights.
  - religious extremism.
  - impeachment.
  - foreign adversaries.
  - staying on message.
- BFF with war criminals & dictators.
- A "Both sides do it" approach to debates & arguments.
- FOX News' favorite Democrat.

LYIN' RYAN

- Masturbates to Ayn Rand quotes.
- Former House Speaker. Ongoing louse.
- Policy: Screw you, I've got mine!
- Ambition: Take the money and run!
- Party over country.
- Workout Bro who needs a Spot!
- Avoids eye contact.
- Represents the will of the 1%.
- Possible kompromat?
- Favorite haircut: The "Eddie Munster."
- Invertebrate.

"I really don't have tremendous political ambition. I have policy ambition."

-- Humble-bragging during a June 2012 Associate Press interview before receiving the GOP's VP nomination.

- Former House Speaker. Ongoing GOP gasbag.
- Family Values paragon currently on 3rd trophy wife.
- Master mold for current set of Republican extremists.
- FOX News rent boy & Tea Party promoter.
- Adulterer who tried to impeach Bill Clinton.
- Contract ON America.
- Sanctimonious opportunist.
- Lobotomized Congress.
- Started trend of shutting down government using hissy fits.

"The thing that shocks people ...is that I mean what I say. I don't use hyperbole."

-- *"Master of Disaster"* by David Beers, *Mother Jones* magazine, Oct 8, 1989.

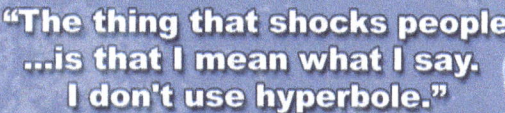

LEWD GINGRICH

HACKABEE

"I didn't major in math. I majored in miracles, and I still believe in them, too."

--- Denying the FACTS that John McCain whupped his ass in Feb. 2008 during the Presidential primaries.

- Worst dad jokes ever.
- "Young Earth" creationist. Old fart.
- Extreme theocratic political ambitions.
- Son has a bad rapport with dogs.
- Daughter has a bad rapport with the truth.
- Ignoramus who claims expertise in science & math.
- Squirrel meat gourmet.
- AKA Chucklebee, The Huckster, Racist Douchebag.
- Former governor, later a talk show host, but always an ongoing right-wing creep ignoring his irrelevancy.

DICK TATOR

- Former self-designated Shadow President.
- Has no heart. Sometimes literally.
- 9/11 was the luckiest day of his life.
- Iraq War criminal. Tops The Hague's "Most Wanted" list.
- Halliburton's Baghdad bag man.
- Chickenhawk who violently mistook a friend for a quail.
- Birth of 1st child (i.e. his 5th deferment) made sure he didn't have to fight in a war he "supported."
- Nixon era relic.
- Torture enthusiast.
- Theme song: The Imperial March.

"Go fuck yourself."

-- To Sen. Patrick Leahy, during an angry exchange on the Senate floor about profiteering by Halliburton, June 25, 2004

The Wrong Side of History's PRESIDENTIAL LIBRARY

U.S. Presidents come & go, leaving lasting **impressions**, chronicled for future generations to study. Some leave *more* than that. Horrendous legacies of **economic disasters**, national **catastrophes**, global **strife**, emotional **trauma**, a **betrayal** of hope & trust, and a whole bunch of other **wacky** sociopolitical shenanigans.

Granted, no President is *perfect*. They're only **human**. They've made, and will make, **mistakes**. Yet, there were some that just **didn't care**. Shameful **opportunists**, lazy **caretakers**, disconnected **careerists**, blatant **criminals**, and all-around **jerks**. Four of the worst within *living memory* of this book's publication date are deconstructed here on this page through the usual *facetious prose* and *badly* researched info punctuated by *snarky* bullet points.

PRICKY DICK
- The Southern Strategy trailblazer.
- Lost the Vietnam War due to his escalating it.
- Set the GOP standard of campaign cheating.
- An inferiority complex dictated his destiny.
- Racist. Mean. Vengeful.
- Fled when Justice was zeroing in.
- *Jesus*, how he hated the Jews!
- The base inspirational muse to the criminals depicted in this book.

THE GIMPER
- 1st *Reality TV* POTUS.
- Union buster.
- Crippled FDR's legacy.
- Ignored the AIDS crisis.
- The Great Obfuscator.
- Trickle-down schemer.
- Deregulated too much.
- Iran-Contra affair.
- The Cold War ended in spite of him.
- The GOP's one true god who, nowadays, would fail their strict purity tests.

PAPA BUSHED
- "Read my lips..."
- '88 campaign amplified ratfucking, attack ads, & racist messaging.
- Gulf War I: CNN's Video Game.
- Pardoned the Iran-Contra cronies.
- The Berlin Wall came down in spite of him.
- Heightened the racist war on drugs.
- Noriega? Saddam? Hide the receipts, Papa!

DUBBLE U
- Radical errorist.
- The politically bad hanging chad.
- Exploited & lied about 9/11.
- Gulf War II: Regime Change for Fun & Profit.
- Dry drunk, born-again hypocrite.
- Hurricane Katrina wiped out his 51% mandate.
- Approved the use of torture.
- Built a housing debt crisis before vacating.
- Unfortunately, he's the 2nd worst President.

@RealDonaldTrump
February 11, 2019:
No president ever worked **harder** than me (cleaning up the mess I inherited)!

DR. KILLMONGER

- Crusty ol' lovable war criminal.
- Idolized/protected by "Very Serious" Institutionalists keeping normalization intact.
- Even he claims his Nobel Peace Prize was undeserved.
- The go-to guy for any Third World based horror between 1969-1977.
- Installer of brutal dictators. Enabler of potential dictators.
- Least favorite book: *The Pentagon Papers*.
- "Madman Theory" architect.
- A cruel, callous a-hole who lived too long.

"The illegal we do immediately; the unconstitutional takes a little longer."

-- From March 10, 1975 meeting with Turkish foreign minister Melih Esenbel in Ankara, Turkey.

RUMMY

"As you know, ah, you go to war with the army you have--- not the army you might want or wish to have at a later time."

--- Rummy's rationalization on why he didn't support the troops. December 2004.

- Regime change prevaricator.
- A not-very-good Defense Secretary.
- International bully.
- Preferred wars on the cheap.
- *The Unknown Known*.
- Pusher of the Iraq-9/11 connection myth.
- Legacy: The radical privatization of the U.S. military.
- Forced American soldiers to adopt a DYI method of combat defense.
- An empty, soulless vessel doing a bad human impersonation.

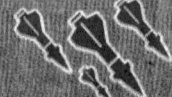

DOUCHE WIT

- Civil liberties lawyer who rationalizes the use of torture.
- Disses the ACLU & Doctors Without Borders.
- Defender for the wealthiest of scum.
- Falsely labeled as a liberal during any brief, open display of a conscience.
- Resorts to "whataboutism" when losing an argument.
- Statutory rape laws crimp his sex life.
- A Rogues' Gallery of clients.
- Persona non grata at any Martha's Vineyard beach party.
- Fair-weather Democrat who chafes at any display of actual Democracy.
- Gets publicly shrill when his social circle gets arrested.
- Mr. Underpants.

"I'm never satisfied unless I get the last word."

— From *Taking the Stand: My Life in the Law.* Another one of his self-serving, pompous books. Published in 2013.

KEN STARRCHAMBER

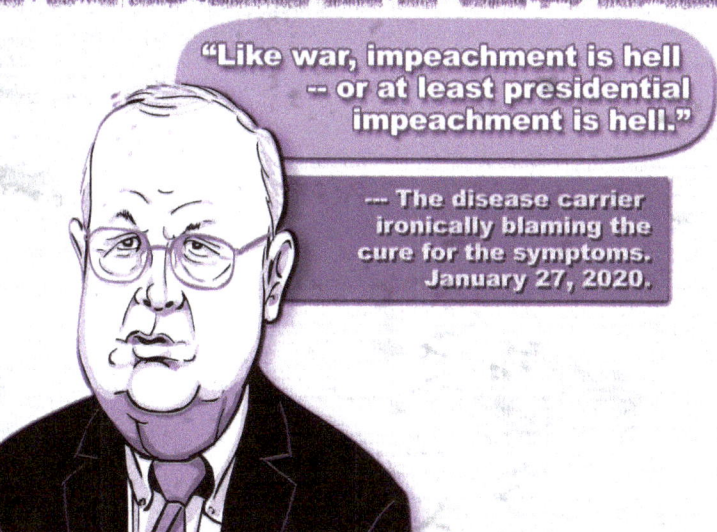

"Like war, impeachment is hell -- or at least presidential impeachment is hell."

--- The disease carrier ironically blaming the cure for the symptoms. January 27, 2020.

- Defines impeachment as a Democrat lying about a blowjob, and nothing else.
- Brett Kavanaugh's former boss.
- Wasted millions of taxpayer dollars back in the '90s to become a laughing stock.
- Partisan hatchet man & political hack.
- Zero scruples.
- Waved away many sexual assault claims while Baylor University president.
- Holy jihad against Godless Liberals explains his lack of principles.
- Supporter of child molesters.
- Jeffrey Epstein's 2007 legal defense.
- Trump's 2020 legal deplorable.

The Wrong Side of History's
IMPEACHMENT GAME

RULES
There ARE NO rules.

THE IDEA OF THE GAME is to BUY the politicians, SELL the messaging, & OWN the law so profitably that one becomes the wealthiest winner and eventual TYRANNICAL OLIGARCH.

A legal defense team BUILDS UP a case based on LIES, DISTORTIONS & DEBUNKED conspiracy theories while TEARING down the CREDIBILITY of the impeachment process & the Constitution for which it stands.

A player goes around the SENATE buying up as much LOYALTY without getting caught. *Cheating* and *Senate Service* cards can be used to assist the player in this agenda.

Once the political body's capability to vote on the matter has been properly CORRUPTED & COMPROMISED, the RIGGING of the trial can proceed, thus ensuring the player will "WIN" the GAME.

Once "ACQUITTAL" has been achieved (EXONERATION is not necessary), then the player's VENDETTA can commence against those DISLOYAL individuals who've been living RENT FREE in the player's head.

The pardoning of CRIMINALS & CRONIES is an added bonus.

THE END GAME is finalized when the RULE OF LAW is broken, JUSTICE is denied, and the RUSSIANS get a return on their investment.

SHYSTER
J. SUCKS LOW

FUNDS FLEECED: $60M+.

- Head of an anti-ACLU crank organization.
- Believes only right wing Christians are defendable.
- *Jews For Jesus* huckster.
- Fundamentalist radio schlock jock.
- Testimony fiction writer.

WHITE HOUSE CONSIGLIERE
PAT SIP A LATTE

"INCOME": $6.7M.

- Former Bill Barr speech-writer.
- Legal inquiry denier.
- Transcript editor of Trump's perfect phone call.
- In the room where it happened.
- Laura Ingraham's buddy.

GAME TOKEN:
CHIEF JUSTICE POTTED PLANT

COUNSEL HYPOCRITE
KEN STARRCHAMBER

COLLECTED NET WORTH: $3M.
COLLECTED CREDIBILITY: N/A.

CLIENTS
2007 Jeffery Epstein.
2008 Proposition 8.
2011 Blackwater.
2020 D. Doll-Hands.

Cheating
YOU'RE FREE TO COMMIT MORE CRIMES

CHECKS AND BALANCES ARE NULL AND VOID

THIS CARD MAY BE KEPT INDEFINITELY BECAUSE JUSTICE IS DEAD

Senate Service
MITT ROMNEY RUINS YOUR PERFECT "ACQUITTAL"

SIC MAGA BOTS ON HIM

HEADS ON PIKES

SYCOPHANT SOLICITOR
JANE RANCOR

FEE (Paid by the RNC): $250K.

- Covering Trump's ass since the Mueller Investigation.
- Underplayed Giuliani's role in extorting Ukraine.
- A legal career spent defending white-collar criminals.

ERIC HUSHMONEY

- Mar-a-Lago legal flunky.
- Clueless to his client's personal history.
- Believes public is also clueless of said history.
- A farcical misrepresentation of facts.

MIKE PURR-PURR

- Donny Doll-Hand's Deputy Counselor.
- LIE 1: No transcript, only a memo.
- LIE 2: Ukraine said no quid pro quo.
- LIE 3: Ukraine didn't know security assistance was paused.
- LIE 4: No witness fingered Trump.
- LIE 5: Trump renewed assistance out of altruism.
- LIE 6: Unlike Obama, Trump was friendlier to Ukraine.

ARROGANT ATTORNEY
BOBBIN RAY

- *Another* Clinton impeachment hypocrite.
- *Another* FOX News favorite.
- Stalked his ex-girlfriend.
- Argued that "abuse of power" is impeachable ...unless it's Trump.
- The George Costanza of lawyers.

Senate Service
COWARDS VOTE TO RIG TRIAL, BUT DON'T EXONERATE YOU

PAY EVERYONE TO APPLAUD

SAD

The Wrong Side of History's
JUDICIAL REVIEW

The Supreme Court is the highest tribunal in the Nation for all cases and controversies arising under the Constitution or the laws of the United States. Ideally, the Court's ultimate responsibility is "Equal justice under law." Throughout America's turbulent history, the Supreme Court has demonstrated certain shortcomings & flaws that failed to meet such promise, proving that no human institution is perfect, immune from bias, or incorruptible.

The years of the early 21st century encapsulated those moments of imperfection. Incompetent, mediocre, and/or intellectually dishonest Justices, chosen for life-long tenure by right-wing Presidents, have the potential to unleash archaic partisan damage, thus keeping a civilization from properly evolving toward a more egalitarian society, where human rights, justice, & the rule of law are available toward everyone, not just a select, wealthy few.

ANTONIN "CULTURE WARRIOR" SCALIA

The tragedy was he died too *late*.

JOHN "EMPTY ROBE" ROBERTS

The useless token piece of the *Impeachment Game*.

ANTHONY "SUDDEN RETIREMENT" KENNEDY

His son approved Trump's Deutsche Bank loan.

SAMUEL "CONSERVATIVE ACTIVIST" ALITO

Gets defensive when the rule of *Citizens United* is challenged.

CLARENCE "COKE CAN" THOMAS

Keeps to a vow of silence as he looks the other way.

NEIL "NOT MERRICK GARLAND" GORSUCH

Placeholder to ensure right-leaning majority votes.

BRETT "PORKY'S REVENGE" KAVANAUGH

Boozy, angry, rape-y white male privilege.

FAUX NEWS

- Trump's favorite propaganda channel ...for now.
- Poisoning the minds of your elderly relatives since 1996.
- Frightwing Noise Machine.
- Lather. Spin. Repeat.
- High paid conspiracy theorists.
- Ruled by a media mogul-o-maniac.
- "We Distort. You Deride."
- A 24/7 Howard Beale fever dream.
- Populated by:
  - Perverted, racist patriarchs.
  - Cruel sex kittens.
  - Rage-fueled revenge harpies.
  - Embarrassing token liberals.
  - Pro-GOP minorities.
  - Bitter, failed comedians.
  - Preening pundit projectionists.

JERKY WATERS — BARON RUPERT — SCREAMIN' JEANINE
LAURA INGRATE — ODD DOBBS
LI'L TUCKER — ROTTEN AILES — TOMAINE
B.O. RILED — THE GIGGLING COUCH TUMORS — SHAMMITY

"Not racist, but #1 with racists."

--- As seen on *The Simpsons* episode "The Fool Monty."
Originally aired Nov. 21, 2010 on the FOX network.

SHAMMITY

- Pusher of debunked conspiracies.
- A Fred Flintstone head packed with prehistoric nonsense.
- FOX News host & parasite.
- "Some people say…"
- Ukrainians on speed dial.
- Aping urbanity. Plump as a manatee.
- Oafish obfuscator.
- Public drama queen, private welfare queen.
- A bloated, jingoistic counterpoint to progress & social justice.
- Trump fluffer.
- Derp state.

"I hate when people use my tactics against me."

-- Responding to a puffball question during a softball interview. "Behind Sean Hannity's Desk" by Mark Anthony Green, *GQ Magazine* Oct. 30, 2011.

LI'L TUCKER

- Bill O'Reilly Lite.
- Idealizes traditional sexism.
- Privileged prep school prick.
- Argument tactics:
  - Blindsiding.
  - False statements.
  - Loaded questions.
  - Badgering.
- ~~Occasionally~~ Constantly spouts white nationalist rhetoric.
- Specializes in self-serving non-apologies.
- Cheerleader of right-wing talking points.
- Professional twerp.

"Most of the time, you can beat a woman in an argument."

-- Expressing his feminist sympathies during an interview from an April 2004 issue of *Elle Magazine*.

SCREAMIN' JEANINE

"It is time to stop being politically correct and start being morally right."

--- CPAC keynote speech emphasizing her sanctimonious hypocrisy. Feb. 24, 2018.

- Crackpot pundit. Failed politician.
- Poster child for Clinton Derangement Syndrome.
- Botoxed Queen of the Damned.
- Ex-district attorney, Ex-judge. Ongoing speed-limit scofflaw.
- Trump's favorite cartoon.
- Channels personal failures via televised shrieks & inebriated slurring.
- Conspired to wiretap her husband.
- Crusader against sex abusers. Now defends the biggest offender.

- Ann Coulter knock-off.
- While at Dartmouth College she:
  - was a *Dartmouth Review* pundit.
  - dated fellow wingnut Dinesh D'Looza.
  - betrayed & outed gay classmates.
- Climate change denier.
- Just *another* racist, fearmongering FOX News Channel host.
- Her brother publicly accused her of being a Nazi sympathizer.
- Ridicules school shooting survivors.
- Likens border detention facilities to "summer camps."
- Homophobe. Transphobe. Xenophobe. Empathy-phobe.

"The more vile the thing that's said about me, the less it affects me. It doesn't bother me at all."

-- The lady doth protested too much on her radio program, methinks. May 26, 2011.

LAURA INGRATE

DINESH D'LOOZA

"A bigot is simply a sociologist without credentials."

-- Meaningless platitude from his laughably naive book *The End of Racism: Principles for a Multiracial Society*. September 1995.

- Convicted launderer of campaign money (Trump's pardon is irrelevant).
- Wife beater with a purple belt in karate.
- Staunch neoconservative & moral hypocrite.
- Birther. Homophobe. Racism rationalist.
- Trolls high school shooting victims.
- Advocate of debunked myths.
- Ronald Reagan necrophiliac.
- Producer of fictional documentaries.
- Determined to prove that people of color can make a career utilizing right-wing nuttery.

- Cruel commentator. Bully pundit.
- Confuses falafels with vibrators.
- Tried to excommunicate ex-wife.
- Wrote *Those Who Trespass*, an unhinged narrative of psychosexual fantasies.
- Wrote *The O'Reilly Factor For Kids*, an unhinged narrative of psychosexual fantasies.
- The Loofah Lothario.
- *War on Christmas* veteran.
- Thin-skinned rage bigot.
- Former FOX News Channel host, current purgatorial podcast pontificator.

"We'll do it live... WE'LL DO IT LIVE! FUCK IT! DO IT LIVE... look, I'll write it and we'll do it live! Fucking thing SUCKS!"

-- Demonstrating professionlism in an outtake from *Inside Edition*. Circa early 1990s.

B.O. RILED

ODD DOBBS

"The idea that a reporter has to be 'fair and balanced' is ridiculous."

-- In an interview with *Radio Ink* magazine October 3, 2005.

- Cranky old man marinating in his debunked conspiracy theories.
- Brain continues to rot from the lead acetate in his shit-brown hair dye.
- Distorts data & news sources to support his archaic, racist views.
- Anti-immigrant advocate who once hired undocumented workers.
- Trump's culture warrior.
- An unstable George Soros obsession.
- Deep State paranoid.
- Hates Republicans who aren't as psychotic & right-wing as he is.
- FOX News Fart.

- Poisonous precious porcelain prevaricator.
- Confuses *Black Lives Matter* with the KKK.
- FOX News blow-up doll.
- Evil eye candy for the morally myopic.
- A female Ann Coulter.
- Anti-feminist both-siderist.
- Second amendment centerfold.
- The worst cosplayer.
- Little Miss Firecracker.
- Slammed ACA while on parents' health insurance plan.
- Wasn't crazy enough for Glenn Beck.
- Thinks peaceful protest is tantamount to treason.
- Final thoughts: Screeds & rants.

"Win on your merit, not your skin color."

-- A hollow "thought" piece re: non-white celebrities. TheBlaze.com January 21, 2016.

TOMAINE

JERKY WATERS

"I am attracted to dumb people."

-- Yukking it up with Bill O at the expense of the less fortunate. *The O'Reilly Factor* December 16, 2013.

- A Fox News Channel smirking dude-bro who failed up as an O'Reilly lackey.
- School yard bully/Racist punk amalgam.
- Laughs at his own cruel, mean jokes.
- His meals continue to have a pungent aftertaste no matter how much he brags about *not* tipping service workers.
- Man-on-the-street ambusher using "gotcha" methods & punching-down humor.
- Mocks his own mother as a shameful ratings grab.
- Hateful harasser of the homeless.
- Gives it, but can't take it.
- Facetious frat boy non-apologist.

- Professional political provocateur & pestilent parasite.
- Her pundit sell-by date has long since expired.
- Historical revisionist.
- Joe McCarthy fangirl.
- Social regressive who denies evolutionary change.
- Her crazy theories have been debunked by fellow right-wingers.
- Believes women shouldn't vote.
- The sense of humor of an impulsive adolescent bully.
- Don't look into her demon eyes---
  Oh no! Aiieeee! (crunching noises)

"Comedy is hard. Any idiot can have an opinion."

-- Explaining in an interview why no one gets her "jokes." POLITICO's Off Message podcast, Sep. 13, 2016.

ANN CRUELTY

RASH LIMBO

"I reject most conventional wisdom."

-- A callous, doughy man implying football players should just walk off their concussions and lifetime injuries. The Rush Limbaugh Show, July 24, 2013.

- He can go very low.
- OxyContin spokesmodel who rails against drug abusers.
- Radio schlock jock & tired novelty act.
- Racist anal cyst.
- Chickenhawk who leads an army of Dittoheads.
- Paranoid right-wing alarmist.
- Maladroit misogynist married 4 times.
- Self-appointed leader of the GOP & other fringe hate groups.
- Decades old source of political vitriol & non-expert ignorance.
- Medal of Freedom fraud.

- Paleoconservative pundit & political dilettante.
- Miserable, tired & archaic Nixon flunky.
- Veteran of the "culture war."
- Most votes gained in a general election: Florida's chaotic butterfly ballot effect.
- Neo-isolationist despising any form of U.S. foreign policy.
- An obvious xenophobe and homophobe.
- Ancient Cold Warrior in agreement with Russia's criminal syndicate agenda.
- Guess how many races & religions he hates!
- Supports the use of torture as interrogation.
- Hey! Guess which sides in the U.S. Civil War & WWII he'd back!

"White America is an endangered species."

-- Dirty old man insisting that white heteros aren't getting laid enough. From his 2011 book *Suicide of a Superpower: Will America Survive to 2025?*

PAT BANANAS

GOLLY G. GIDDY

"Go for a head shot; they're going to be wearing bulletproof vests."

-- His advice on how to kill federal agents. Spoken on his own radio show while using the public airwaves. August 26, 1994.

- He's got... lifeless eyes, black eyes, like a doll's eyes.
- Leader of a third-rate burglary ring.
- A Machiavellian menace.
- Nixon's top plumber and ratfucker.
- Barbecued his own hand for fun.
- Jailbird who capitalized from his dirty dealings.
- Two-bit actor who usually played two-bit versions of himself.
- Antisemitic supporter of Israel because "biblical end-times" shit.
- Radio show host who ranted about the usual wingnut, reactionary nonsense.

The Wrong Side of History's
CORPORATE MEDIA

A Democracy depends on a free and independent press to hold the government accountable as well as informing, educating & enlightening the citizens so they can properly engage and participate in a civilized society.

That's not possible in a country overrun by capitalism and corruption, where large, monolithic corporations own & control the messaging put forth by their infotainment cartel.

Displayed here is an assembled panel of mediocre, overpaid, lazy commentators, producers, personalities, and columnists who fail in their public responsibilities. Pushers of inferior journalism, bad faith arguments, news as entertainment, bilateralism and harmful objectivity, enabling cruel, greedy people & organizations to wield undeserved, unaccountable power.

- *Meet The Press* placeholder.
- Boyish both-siderist.
- Mediocre debate moderator.
- Journalist after the fact.
- Why is he on TV?

NEBBISH

SHUCKS TODD (Cub Reporter)

• Realized his political naiveté too little, too late. •

- Insistent normalizers.
- Pay no attention to their 2016 election coverage.
- Never-Trumpers who didn't see it coming.
- "...stunningly superficial knowledge..."
  -- Zbigniew Brzezinski
  December 30, 2008

GET A ROOM!

STATUS JOE & M'KAY (Codependents)

Pushers of the debunked "DNC rigged the primaries" mem

- Professional talk sho-- *Interrupter!*
- Played "hardball" right-of-center.
- No impulse control.
- The Dunning-Kruger effect of social graces.
- Flannelmouthed lightning rod.

TWEETY

CHRIS MAD-NEWS (Quasi-Liberal)

• He took a minute & a huff to leave his final show. •

- CNN's "empty podium" promoter.
- Backpedaling Trump enabler.
- Cynical, vacant ratings merchant.
- Trivializes serious political issues.
- Turned America into a bad reality TV show.

HUMAN POTATO

JEFF HUCKSTER (Conflict Profiteer)

Cable news president feeding on cronyism & mendacity.

The Wrong Side of History's CORPORATE MEDIA

@RealDonaldTrump
October 4, 2017:
Wow, so many Fake News stories today. No matter what I do or say, they will not write or speak truth. The Fake News Media is out of control!

FART SNIFFER
BOBO BROOKS (Pop Psychologist)
- Conservative fantasist.
- Always spectacularly wrong.
- Condescending snob.
- Red state whisperer.
- "Third-wave feminist."
- George W Bush fanboy.
- *NY Times* anti-journalist; All the opinion that's shit to print.

WHINER
CHRIS SLEEZZA (Know-Nothing)
- CNN's resident idiot.
- Always reliably wrong.
- Gripe tweets about his high-paying job.
- Former intern to snooty George Will.
- Unserious infotainment passing as analysis.
- *The Po!nt* being, he doesn't know crap.

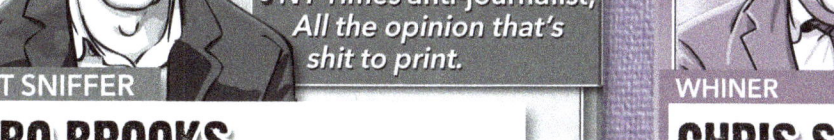
Practiced in the art of Tasteful Objection tautology. • Defends political theater and "horserace" journalism.

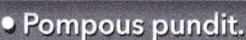

CREEPY
HUGE SPEWITT (Partisan Hack)
- Pompous pundit.
- Trump loyalist.
- CEO of the Richard Nixon Foundation.
- Iraq War booster.
- Pusher of the archaic "liberal media" trope.
- Hannity wannabe.
- Defends the indefensible.

CLUELESS
JONAH HAMBERG (Doughy Pantload)
- Arrogant bloviator.
- Nepotism beneficiary.
- Thinks liberals are fascists.
- A living logical fallacy.
- His politics shift with the times
- Conservative writer, commentator, jerk.

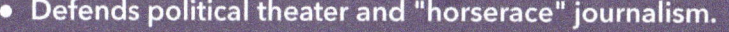
Claimed the legal impeachment of Trump was a "coup." • His mom touched off the Monica Lewinsky scandal

GNARLED ROVE

- AKA: Turdblossom. Bush's Brain. The Architect.
- From dweeby Young Republican to dumpy political pundit.
- Dirty tricks he pioneered/enhanced:
  - Fake grassroots PAC groups spreading untruths.
  - The "swiftboating" of war heroes.
  - Bugged his own office to garner sympathy.
  - Planting "reporters" to ask rigged questions.
  - Political judo: Projection to deflect from real issues.
- Rampant homophobe who may be hiding something *personal* (Google: Jeff Gannon).
- Fled his WH staff job in 2007 when the subpoenas started flying.
- 2012 election finally exposed him as a washed-up political charlatan.

"We will fuck him. Do you hear me? We will fuck him. We will ruin him. Like no one has ever fucked him!"

-- A quiet moment of introspection as witnessed by journalist Ron Suskind. "Why Are These Men Laughing?" Esquire magazine, January 2003.

RICK SANSCROTUM

"I don't want to make black people's lives better by giving them somebody else's money; I want to give them the opportunity to go out and earn the money."

-- Rhetorical dogwhistles on the campaign trail to an all white crowd in Iowa. January 2012.

- Former U.S. Representative & Senator.
- Failed Presidential candidate.
- Frothy weirdo & blathering talking head.
- Smug, self-righteous fundamentalist.
- Tried inserting "intelligent design" and other anti-science claptrap into the 2001 "No Child Left Behind" bill.
- Stupid things he compares consensual homosexuality with: beastiality, bigamy, incest, adultery, & anything else that gives him a secret, sinful erection.
- Believed WMDs were in Iraq, despite reality proving otherwise.
- Racist. "Pro-life." Climate denier. Ass.

- Contradicting Both-Siderist.
- Professional Equivocator.
- Non-credentialed journalist.
- Self-appointed chaos agent.
- Confuses criticism about him as acts of censorship.
- Disruption is his brand.
- Intellectual bully.
- Trump-Russia denier.
- Obfuscates serious news stories with sloppy personal conjectures.
- Pseudo progressive passing as a Purity Left leader.
- Suffers from an irony deficiency.

"My inbox is the enemy."

-- Self-important boast about his email account. "Snowden and Greenwald: The Men Who Leaked the Secrets." *RollingStone* magazine. December 4, 2013.

GLENN GRIEVANCE

MATTED SLUDGE

"And you would be amazed what the ordinary guy knows... every citizen can be a reporter."

-- From a June 2, 1998 National Press Club speech ironically making the argument for editorial gatekeepers.

- Telemarketer turned low budget Walter Winchell.
- Citizen "reporter." Online gossip.
- Prose style: Stream-of-consciousness drivel & random ramblings.
- Sell by date expired after 1999.
- His poorly designed website...
  - Aggregates links to confabulations and racist dog whistles.
  - Artificially inflates visitor count.
- Booster of birtherism and climate change denial.
- Ruined the fedora as a serious hat for generations to come.

APOPLEX JONES

- The Human Thumb of Insanity.
- Modern snake oil salesman.
- Conspiracy theorist & rage-aholic.
- Alternative reality Info Warrior.
- Survivalist pitchman.
- High-functioning aneurysm.
- The Godfather of Fake News.
- Paranoid pantopragmatic.
- False flag waver & Pseudohistorian.
- Trump whisperer.
- For some reason, lost custody of his kids in a court case.

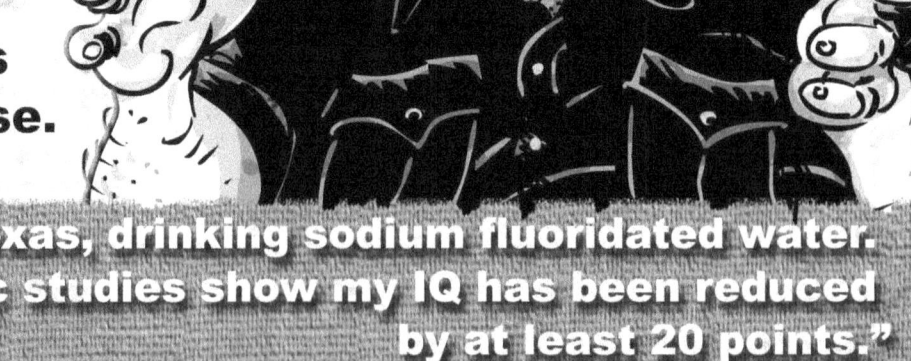

"I grew up in Dallas, Texas, drinking sodium fluoridated water. All the scientific studies show my IQ has been reduced by at least 20 points."

-- From his banned YouTube video *Question Your Reality.* February 11, 2008.

WEIRD MIKE

- Info Warrior who just figured out how fire & the wheel works.
- Professional Concern Troll.
- Anti-Trans. Pro-Rape.
- Perversion Projectionist.
- *Pizzagate* delivery boy.
- Gish Galloping Goon.
- *Gorilla Mindset* scam.
- All-Wrong Alt-Right.
- Supported by alimony from rich ex-wife.
- Putin taint-licker.
- Gamergate legal counsel.
- It's all about him.

"Why are you OBSESSED with me when you hate me? Seems like you should make better use of your time."

-- Defensive, petulant non-answer during his Reddit AMA session. December 22, 2017.

SPENCER GRIFTS

"We hold these truths to be self-evident; that all men are created unequal."

-- From an unfunny blog article "The Metapolitics of America." RadixJournal.com July 4, 2014.

- A face that is the target of many a righteous fist.
- Collector of hateful lapel pins.
- Neo-Nazi novelty item.
- President of a white nationalist "think" tank.
- Privileged, pampered man-child.
- Whiner about imaginary "white genocide."
- Hairstyle: The Hitler Youth High & Tight-ass.
- Cringe-worthy creep.
- Feeds off his own chaos.
- Mentioning he's racist & antisemitic would be redundant.

- Preening pissant peacock & petulant provocateur.
- Professional victim.
- Advocate of pederasty.
- Former Breitbart "journalist."
- Supports & promotes the most ridiculous of conspiracies.
- Perpetual adolescent who claims his homosexuality is just a phase.
- Gamergate courtier.
- Social media pariah.
- Too toxic for CPAC.
- Deemed a harmful species by the Australian government.

"I like to think of myself as a virtuous troll."

-- On ABC News' *Nightline* rationalizing his vicious Twitter stalking of performer Leslie Jones. Sept. 1, 2016.

MOFO YAWNOPOLIS

JACOB DROLL

"Make shit up. ... Leak something sensational, extreme, sexual, scandalous, trending, or hate triggering."

-- Part of his "sales pitch" to ~~suckers~~ investors on ways to spread lies & fake news during the 2020 elections. April 30, 2019.

- Little boy with big dreams & no clue.
- Failed blogger & gossipmonger.
- Perpetrator of implausible scandals.
- Holds blundering, comical press briefings.
- Business # is mother's phone #.
- Associate Jack Burkman suffers from wardrobe malfunctions.
- Charged with the crime of investment fraud.
- Fantasizer of Trump-lovin' hipster coffee shops.
- Too unstable even for *The Gateway Pundit*.
- Surefire Irrelevance.

- Right-wing squeak toy & dog whistle.
- Professional idiot.
- Another fragile, easily triggered, straight, white conservative.
- Claims not to be racist, but…
- Virulent transphobe.
- Climate change denier flaunting his non-expert expertise.
- *Sesame Street* is brought to you by the letter L …for LEFTY & LIBERAL!
- Declares victory in an argument via the ad hominem attack.
- Claims to be #NeverTrump, but…

"We are watching our civilisation collapse into age-old tribalism, individualistic hedonism, and moral subjectivism."

-- Unprovable, opinionated claptrap from his humorously entitled book *The Right Side of History: How Reason and Moral Purpose Made the West Great*. March 2019.

BEAN SHAPE

CHARLIE SMIRK

"Obviously we reject any foreign adversary using any content. Russia is an enemy of the state."

-- Facetious backpedaling when told that TPUSA's lies & propaganda were being put to viral use in 2016. *Business Insider*, January 5, 2019.

- Another dim-witted MAGA grifter.
- Head of *Turning Point USA*, a youth organization dedicated to political immaturity & boozy rape.
- Concern trolls socialists for having an iPhone & wifi access.
- Griped about high school textbooks on economics having a "liberal bias."
- Argues in bad faith about atheism.
- Intense partisan hypocrite.
- Misinformation meme generator misreading his entire generation.
- Crybaby who actually protested wearing a diaper.

The Wrong Side of History's
UNSTABLE ELEMENTS

Beyond the safe, commercial confines of mainstream media lies the dark hinterlands of disinformed *wingnuttery*, destructive *opinions*, and barbaric *buffoonery* populated by many selfish **grifters** & diseased **egos**. Granted, that's most of this book's **content**. There are just too many of these *horrible creatures* to properly deconstruct and **dissect** for deserved **mockery**. Assembled on these pages is a miscellaneous *psyche profile* dredged up from America's conspiratorial **primal id**.

J.O. QUEEFE
- Hidden camera conman.
- Self-important sleazoid.
- Project Veritas = Virtual agitprop.
- Criminal who never learns a lesson.
- Sloppy "sting" methods.
- Tried to prove voter fraud by committing it!
- Enemy of institutes that assist the poor & less fortunate.

GLIB BLECH
- Profits off his personal paranoia & crocodile tears.
- Clownish commentator.
- Espouses only the best of crazy conspiracy theories.
- Aged like a fine whiner made from sour grapes.
- "End Times" enthusiast.
- Frothy fear fomenter.
- Goldbug huckster.
- Firebug who started *TheBlaze*.

MARK LIVID
- Hate radio "personality".
- Vocalizes many a stupid thing in the worst voice possible.
- Another NeverTrump-er who drank the orange Kool-Aid.
- Practiced in the art of the uncivil discourse.
- Dim-witted "Deep State" diatribes.
- Insane observations:
  - Same-sex marriage = incest.
  - U.S. *not* a nation of immigrants. ...wtf...?

MIKE SEWAGE
- Another right-wing a-hole stereotype with a mic.
- His real last name is Weiner!
- Your standard liberal demonizer.
- Claims he was raised "...on neglect, anger and hate."
- Vitriolic, toxic masculinity.
- Stochastic terrorist banned for life from the U.K.
- An argument style based on screams, insults, & threats.
- Political views inspired by his delusional disorders.

The Wrong Side of History's UNSTABLE ELEMENTS

@RealDonaldTrump October 29, 2018:
There is great anger in our Country caused in part by inaccurate, and even fraudulent, reporting of the news. The Fake News Media, the true Enemy of the People, must stop the open & obvious hostility & report the news accurately & fairly. That will do much to put out the flame...

- A self-described "investigative journalist."
- Owner of many a defunct domain name.
- A cheap Karl Rove knock-off.
- Dox-ter Schlocktopus.
- Banned from Twitter.
- Provides no evidence in his accusations.
- Wikileaks liaison.
- Teddy Ruxpin gone horribly wrong.

UPCHUCKY

- Supporters of white racists.
- P.R. props for white racists.
- Nutty neo-con vloggers.
- Evil mirror universe version of comedy duo *Frangela*.
- Trump fan girls.
- Right-wing media darlings.
- Confederate statues: Yes.
- Gun control: No.
- Their persecution complex is all a LEFTIST PLOT!

ZIRCONIUM & POLYESTER

- "You betcha!"
- Caribou Barbie.
- Reality TV show star.
- John McCain's regrettable decision.
- Not a very good teacher of abstinence.
- Homecoming queen with a gun.
- Quit as Alaska Governor to avoid legal investigations.
- The political portent of Donny Doll-Hands.

SARAH FAILIN'

- Lunatic chickenhawk & has-been rocker.
- Pseudopatriot pedophile.
- Gun nut who threatened the lives of elected officials.
- Racist appropriating the legacy of black musicians.
- Cowardly hunter who gets off on suffering.
- Cat Scratch Pervert.
- Just another redneck a-hole.

TED NOUGAT

Nutjobs ★ Relics ★ Assholes

- US Domestic terrorist organization.
- Guns don't kill people. Bullets tearing through flesh kill people.
- Supported by WhatAbout-isms & False Equivalencies.
- Roadblock to prosperity, progress & peace.
- Feeds off fear, chaos & ignorance.
- Arming psychopaths for the greater GREED.
- Accepts donations in rubles.
- Misinterprets the 2nd Amendment.
- No tyrants overthrown yet.
- Archaic & irrelevant since the end of the 19th century.
- The GOP's favorite special interest.
- All together now: PENIS!

"...the right of the people to keep and bear Arms, shall not be infringed."

-- The second half of the 2nd Amendment emblazoned across the front of the NRA's Washington D.C. HQ. No need for that inconvenient, pesky "well regulated Militia" reference.

- Violent tragedy profiteer.
- Professional scapegoater, finger-pointer & blame thrower.
- Leader of Nutjobs, Relics, Assholes.
- Sacrifices lives of fellow citizens for the sake of an archaic amendment.
- Defends gun manufacturers from the consequences of their products' actions.
- Bad guy with a gun lobby.
- Gun control laws could stop him from shooting off his own mouth.
- Fits profile of "crazed loner."

"We can't lose precious time debating legislation that won't work."

-- Insensitive, inhuman response to the tragic mass school shooting in Newtown, CT. December 21, 2012.

WAYNE LaPARIAH

DANA LASH-OUT

"Many in legacy media love mass shootings. You guys love it."

-- At CPAC playing the blame game to rationalize gun violence. February 21, 2018.

- Spewer of fake gun facts, lies, vitriol, spittle.
- Sancti-Mommy-ous hypocrite whose amorality threatens other people's children.
- A walking Freudian subtext.
- Professional Mean Girl who loses high school debates.
- 2nd Amendment Apologist.
- NRA spokesperson & faux outrage harpy.
- Tea Party co-founder.
- Star of pro-gun snuff videos.
- Revolutionary War Revisionist.

- Menacing Mercenaries-R-Us.
- Seychelles "tourist".
- *Focus on the Family* fanboy.
- Known to snuff out whistleblowers.
- Former intern to Congressman Dana "Putin Pal" Rohrabacher.
- Betsy DeVos' creepy little brother.
- Fancies himself a modern day Christian Crusader.
- Weapons smuggler.
- Cambridge Analytica ally.
- Favorite boyhood memory: Visiting concentration camp sites in Germany.

"Don't get me started on the State Department."

-- A momentary reveal on how much he hates the concept of diplomacy. "Blackwater's Erik Prince On How He Got Into The White House" Huffpost.com August 31, 2017.

PRINCE BLACKWATER

JUDGE ROY BOY

"It would bother me if a judge told me how I had to believe."

-- A deflecting non-answer during an interview on PBS's *Flashpoints USA* with Bryant Gumbel and Gwen Ifill. January 27, 2004.

- Ten Commandments fanatic.
- US Constitution denier.
- High school yearbook signer.
- Darling of the Deplorables.
- He & the wife just love them "jeewwws."
- Theocratic thug.
- Homophobe. Racist. Creep.
- Faux cowboy.
- Pistol-packin' pedophile.
- Exiled mall rat.
- Possible Russian sleeper agent.
- Hated by horses.
- Pathetic sore loser.

- Terrorized Maricopa County, AZ for 24 lawless years.
- Trump's "pardon" emphasized just how guilty he was.
- Master of the false arrest.
- Unconstitutionally cruel jails.
- Sadly faked an assassination attempt on himself to garner voter sympathy.
- Taxpayer-funded self-promotions.
- Ignored over 400 sexual assault cases.
- Wild west vigilante style of justice.
- Anti-immigrant racist. Gosh, no surprise there.

"Well you know, they call you KKK. They did me. I think it's an honor. It means we're doing something."

-- Taking pride in his abuse of civil rights during an interview on CNN's *Lou Dobbs Tonight*. November 12, 2007.

BOSS J. AHOLE
SHERIFF CRACKED

"First of all, there is no police brutality in America. We ended that back in the '60s."

-- Comfortably lying from a safe location. *Fox & Friends*, October 26, 2015.

- Wingnut conservative firebrand.
- DINO who cynically exploited the Democrat-leaning electorate of Milwaukee, WI for 15 years.
- Supervised an abusive jail with lethal water rationing as punishment.
- A vocal critic of *Black Lives Matter*.
- Flamboyantly dressed homophobe.
- Hoarder of *many* medals, pins & buttons.
- 2015 Moscow trip funded by the NRA.
- Authoritative hatred of *habeas corpus*.
- Too nutty for Trump's administration.

REV. PATRONIZE

- All sins are forgivable once the checks clear.
- Misanthropic Methuselah.
- Proof that a sane, benevolent God doesn't exist.
- Opposes anything that assists, enlightens, educates, or advances society.
- Old school TV preacher.
- Old school ...everything!
- Christian Charlatan.
- Name the tragedy, he'll blame the victims.
- False prophet profiting from fear, doubt, hate & stupidity.
- 700 Club: His age group.

"I have a zero tolerance for sanctimonious morons who try to scare people."

-- Yep. He said it. When and where is not verifiable, but the quote was cited in an April 15, 2011 *Washington Post* article *"Liberals pride themselves on being tolerant. Are they really just suckers?"* by Sally Kohn.

THE FALLINHELLS

- Moral Majority Christofascist & his sniveling legacy spawn.
- Founded/runs "Liberty University" & all of its Orwellian doublethink.
- Senior made a fool of himself:
  - blaming 9/11 on homosexuals, pagans, & feminists.
  - waging "war" on *Hustler* magazine & *The Teletubbies*.
- Junior made a fool of himself:
  - "supporting" his blackmailer Trump.
  - mentoring pool boys for fun & profit.
  - exposing L.U. students & staff to COVID-19.
- Fundamentalists preaching & teaching:
  - Pseudoscience.
  - Young Earth Creationism.
  - Biblical Dumbfuckery 101.

"The idea that religion and politics don't mix was invented by the Devil to keep Christians from running their own country."
-- Senior's Bicentennial sermon preaching anti-Constitutional fairytale logic. July 4, 1976.

"I see a lot of parallels between my father and Donald Trump."
-- Junior confessing his Daddy issues in front of a captive L.U. crowd. January 18, 2016.

SENIOR (ROTTING DEAD)
JUNIOR (WALKING DEAD)

FRANKLIN GRANDIOSE

"Just being the son of Billy Graham won't get me into heaven."
-- Realizing his life is a lie & he's going to Hell. *Rebel with a Cause: Finally Comfortable Being Graham* 1995.

- Another sad mediocre living in a long, paternal shadow & coming up short.
- Idiot Islamophobe lacking faith in the strength of his own religion to coexist with another.
- Putin's anti-gay laws are A-OK with his narrow world-view.
- Confederate statue preservationist.
- Defender of Republican perverts.
- Cherry-picker of Christian values.
- Accused *Christianity Today*, founded by his own father, of liberal elitism.
- Mr. Ratburn's wedding crasher.

The Wrong Side of History's
SELFISH BEHAVIOR

Whereas most religions or secular philosophies can be used for either good or evil, creativity or destruction, Objectivism caters only to the terrible traits of humanity. Growing like a cancer since the latter half of the 20th century, Objectivism's contribution to the sociopolitical strata of modern civilization has caused much irreparable damage.

This hateful rhetoric romanticizes the limited concepts of "greed is good," "me first," & "screw you, I've got mine" over the altruistic notions of providing for the common defense, promoting the general welfare & securing the blessings of liberty. In other words, it's the general maxim of perpetually immature me-monkeys who see nothing wrong in establishing goals that can cause long-term public chaos for short-term personal, private gain.

"It relates to business (and) beauty (and) life and inner emotions. That book relates to ... everything." -- Donny Doll-Hands bigly gushing about *The Fountainhead*, a book he probably just heard about that day. *USA Today* April 10, 2016.

AYN RANCID
- Author of thick, boring books.
- Fan girl of serial killers.
- Her bad adolescence is now part of society's burden.
- Anti-socialist who became an aged welfare queen.
- Not a friend to feminism.
- Narcissitic laissez-faire capitalist.
- Rationalized asshole-ry.
- Inspired generations of spiteful know-nothings to wreak havoc upon the world through avarice & rapacious dumbness.

RANDOM & WRONG PALL
Father & son comedy act linking their careers to a bad joke.

RON "THE CON" JOHNSON
Atlas Shrugged laid the foundation for his mediocre villainy.

LYIN' RYAN
Loved the greedy cruelty, not so much the pro-choice/atheism aspect.

PETER SPIEL
Vulture capitalist yearning to feast on the carcass of free speech.

CLARENCE "COKE CAN" THOMAS
Forces his law clerks to watch *The Fountainhead*.

ALAN GREEDSPAN
Dedicated acolyte who applied horrible, fictional rhetoric to real world finances, resulting in disasterous, long-term damage.

THE GIMPER
Big admirer of Ayn's work. She didn't return the sentiment.

KOCHTOPUS

- Multi-tentacled money monster.
- Novelty brother act well past its sell-by date.
- Avoids bright lights & documentary exposés.
- Libertarian think tank funders & septic tank dwellers.
- Uses philanthropy as way to inject venom into victims.
- Any destructive moment linked to politics, culture, infrastructure, environment, industry or transportation over the last 60 years. That's probably them.
- Any deathly stench linked to a blurry shadow skittering by. That's probably them, too.

"We'd like to abolish the Federal Elections Commission and all the limits on campaign spending anyway."

-- David regarding contributions of $100K a month to his own Libertarian Vice Presidential campaign. *New York* Magazine, November 3, 1980.

"I don't want to dedicate my life to getting publicity."

-- Charles getting snippy when his family's scheming gets exposed to the light. "Pulling the Wraps Off Koch Industries," *New York Times*, November 20, 1994.

THE IMMERSERS

- Bankrolled Breitbart, Brexit, Cambridge Analytica, & other harmful brain parasites.
- Don't stare at their weird heads.
- Claim black people were better off before Civil Rights.
- In favor of the gold standard.
- Pseudoscience funders.
- Geez! Those heads!
- Easily fooled by conspiracy theorists.
- Emulating bad human traits: racism, greed, vanity, etc.
  ...but they're NOT aliens!

R-BERT   **R-BEKAH**

"To be like the hu-man! To laugh! Feel! Want! Why are these things not in the plan?"

-- Ro-Man, the titular alien featured in the film *Robot Monster* (1953)

BARON RUPERT

- Purveyor of perversion, scandal, fake news & moral decay.
- AKA "The Dirty Digger."
- Wanted on 3 continents for the savage slaughter of credible journalism.
- Proof that the good die young.
- News Corp chairman & old corpse.
- Media philosophy: Fear, Doubt, Hate, & Tits.
- The Dumbing-downer from Down Under.
- Another wealthy, miserable bastard poisoning the wellspring of humanity because he can.

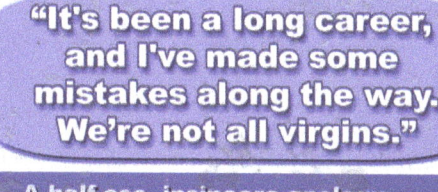

"It's been a long career, and I've made some mistakes along the way. We're not all virgins."

– A half-ass, insincere apology from a *Time* magazine interview, July 2007.

SHELF-LIFE ADELSON

"I've already figured out when I'm going to be No. 2 and No. 1."

– His personal dick-measuring contest in trying to be the richest asshole. *Los Angeles Times*, Sep. 28, 2006.

- Billionaire GOP megadonor & pustulate bowl of pudding.
- Unhinged, unscrupulous, anti-union unguent.
- Funded the diplomatic no-no of moving US Embassy for Israel from Tel Aviv to Jerusalem.
- Enabler of gambling addicts.
- Stiffs contractors for fun.
- Loves to frivolously sue.
- Briber extraordinaire.
- The more money he hoards, the more his head recedes into his chest cavity.

- Self-made monster.
- A very large AMBER Alert archive file.
- Hosted Trump's most fondled memories.
- Bill Barr's dad was a résumé reference.
- The social disease of celebrities, politicians, & other nervous people.
- A badly outsourced autoerotic asphyxia prison fantasy?
- A suspicious amount of wealth vs. a suspicious lack of wealth.
- Hedge funder, corporate raider, & Ponzi schemer.
- Hired ex-girlfriend as a pimp.
- Professional blackmailer.
- The Tell-Tale Corpse.

"I like to hear voices and see faces when I interact."

-- Regarding how he did his business ...& his "business." *Jeffrey Epstein: International Moneyman of Mystery,"* by Landon Thomas, Jr. *New York* magazine, October 28, 2002.

JEFFENSTEIN

PERVY WISENHEIM

"All my movies got screwed up because of my personality."

-- Being self-aware when it mattered, but not where it counted. *Down and Dirty Pictures: Miramax, Sundance, and the Rise of Independent Film,* by Peter Biskind 2004.

- Damager of film industry careers.
- A creepy, deviant Venn Diagram of entertainment & politics.
- The right-wing's go-to morality shibboleth & subject changer.
- The horrific plot device of many a Hollywood #MeToo narrative.
- A manipulative bully.
- A loud predator who flourished in a culture of silence.
- Exploiter/Violator of trust.
- Movie producer. Rapist.

- Coal baron & SLAPP suit specialist.
- As a human mole there's nothing's beneath him.
- Took business advice from a squirrel.
- Enemy's list:
  - Editorial cartoonists.
  - Polite protesters.
  - Small town newspapers.
  - HBO, John Oliver, & Mr. Nutterbutter.
- Blamed tragic mine collapse not on his company's neglect & incompetency, but on an imaginary earthquake.
- Black lung's biggest defender.
- "Eat shit, Bob!" - Employee commentary.
- Industrial polluter clinging to his asshole-ry.
- Dirty old man, in so many ways.

"...so-called global warming is a total hoax."

-- Dinosaur unaware of what a fossil fool he is. "Trump May 'Dig' Coal, But Industry's Outlook Is Flat at Best," by Tim Loh. Bloomberg News November 10, 2016.

BOB MOLEMAN

MARTY SKULKY

"I don't mean to be presumptuous, but I liken myself to the robber barons."

-- Being obnoxiously presumptuous in a Vanity Fair article. December 18, 2015.

- Smug millionaire turned pouty jailbird.
- A loathsome, punchable face.
- Wall Street hedge funding creep.
- Price gouger of life-saving drugs.
- Wu-Tang Clan's least-favorite fan.
- Looks like a dummy that just killed its ventriloquist.
- Threatened former employee's family.
- His lawyer called him a "genius." He forgot the "evil" preface.
- Pharma Bro justifiably bitch-slapped by karma, yo.
- Once deemed "America's Most Hated Individual." Simpler times.

The Wrong Side of History's SILICON AVATARS

Robber barons & plutocrats of old exploited the industrial revolution & worked it to their selfish advantage for decades until economies & cultures collapsed from their hubris.

The modern world suffers through a second Gilded Age, one that's digitally-enhanced. Petulant, greedy technocrats abuse the trust of online citizens & the internet-dependent masses relying on an app system promising to make life quicker, responsive, & possibly more convenient.

This cybernetic infrastructure has progressive, enlightening potential, but it can never reach that goal if a small percentage of billionaire I.T. geeks keep shaking things up with all the foresight of a cruel 8 year old clutching an ant farm.

FACE ZUCK

Artificial Intelligence that would fail the Turing Test.

- The Dr. Frankenstein of social media.
- Offered "free internet" to rural India via Facebook-only portal.
- Claimed privacy dead as he bought up miles of property around his houses.
- Emoji-like emotional depth.
- Lost Boy of a technocratic Neverland.
- Kept mum about Cambridge Analytica apps.
- Privileged chaos agent.

J@CK DOOZY

Hashtagging hot mess.

- Creator of Trump's favorite bully pulpit. #complicit.
- Handles Twitter trolls by way of a "Blame the victim" motif. #amoral
- Fad diet practitioner with an unhealthy amount of free time. #eatingdisorders
- Isolated tech bro incapable of adulting. #irresponsible
- An empty vessel in which 140 to 280 characters cannot fill. #deadinside

PETER SPIEL

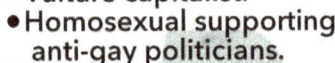

False profit Libertarian.

- Vulture capitalist.
- Homosexual supporting anti-gay politicians.
- Co-founded PayPal. It prospered *after* he sold his shares.
- Palantir, his data-spying firm, is named after an artifact used for evil in *The Lord of the Rings*.
- Pseudoscience proponent.
- Funded the *Hulk Hogan v. Gawker* lawsuit in order to settle a personal grudge. Set an eerie precedent for censorship.

JEFF BAZILLION

The Lex Luthor of Earth Prime delivery.

- If he:
  - Paid employees a living wage,
  - Provided warehouse safety,
  - Paid his fuckin' taxes,
  - Stopped being a comic book super-villain,

  he'd still be a wealthy prick.
- Brutal control freak.
- A damn good reason for Democratic Socialism.
- Predatory attitude toward small book publishers.
- Amazon swoop logo: His penis.

J. ASS ANGER

- Scene stealer. Attention whore.
- WikiLiar.
- ~~Enemy~~ Darling of US right-wingers.
- Russia's favorite propagandist.
- Pretender of impartiality.
- Conspiracy fabulist.
- Hobbies:
  - Backpedaling.
  - Self-vindication.
  - Jumping young women/bail.
- Learned to hate Ecuadorian cuisine.
- Living Troll Meme.
- Bragged about his released leaks & massive dumps.

"These big-package releases. There should be a cute name for them."

-- *This Machine Kills Secrets: Julian Assange, the Cypherpunks, and Their Fight to Empower Whistleblowers* by Andy Greenberg, Sept. 2012. Back when his chaos agent crap was being naively romanticized.

NIGEL FOLDEROL

"I don't listen to music. I don't watch television, I don't read."

-- Expressing why he's so *relatable* to the general voting public. *"Voice of Ukip: Nigel's Making Plans For Us,"* by Rachel Cooke. *The Observer* magazine, March 29, 2015.

- Upper Class Twit contest winner.
- UKIP. Brexit. Git. Pillock. Tosser.
- Feeds off racism & divisiveness.
- Wanks off to WikiLeaks.
- FBI's "Person of Interest."
- Credit stealer.
- Putin admirer. Trump booster.
- Responsibility shirker.
- Offensively dispassionate.
- Promise breaker.
- Tax-payer funded EU pension recipient.
- Culturally deprived.
- *V For Vendetta* villain.

LORD BOORISH

- Political bowl of over-cooked pudding.
- The "clever," British Donald Trump.
- Brexit in a fright wig.
- Schmoozy wannabe authoritarian.
- Diverts from real issues via aggressive niceness & off-putting buffoonery.
- Drove around UK in a German-made bus spreading lies about the EU.
- Former Foreign Secretary who offended many a country.
- The first UK PM who will finally succeed at blowing up Parliament.
- Pooh-poohed COVID-19 until it kicked his arse.

"My chances of being PM are about as good as the chances of finding Elvis on Mars, or my being reincarnated as an olive."

-- In response to a citizen's query in the "You Ask The Questions" section of the UK paper *The Independent*, June 17, 2004.

KID YOUNG'UN

- North Korea's "Little Brother" "born" in 1984.
- Continues the family tradition of rewriting history, making shit up, & crushing the dreams of his people.
- Doesn't play favorites. Kills minions & relatives with the same zeal.
- Vengeful film critic for the DPRK.
- As Trump's BFF they share:
  - funny nicknames.
  - broken promises.
  - inhuman cruelty mixed with cartoonish élan.
  - daddy issues.
  - odd hairstyles.
  - weird body shapes.
  - brain damage.
- Nuclear dick waver.

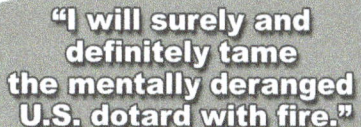

"I will surely and definitely tame the mentally deranged U.S. dotard with fire."

-- A public "love letter" reply to his favorite authoritarian-wannabe. September 22, 2017.

MSG

"I fear that the day I die, I am going to die without accomplishing what I have in my mind."

-- Getting away with his bullshit in an ass-kissing *New York Times* article by Thomas Friedman. November 23, 2017.

- Saudi crown prince/dictator trainee.
- Wants to modernize his culture by:
  - criminalizing online satire,
  - allowing women to drive so they can be arrested for whole new reasons,
  - hacking up journalists with chainsaws instead of scimitars.
- The next generation of Middle East turmoil.
- Propping up Al-Qaeda & DAESH while ruling a country that funded 9/11.
- Building up a war crime tally with his youthful exuberance.
- Beloved by Trump & other right-wingers.
- Power consolidation inspired by Putin playbook.

COMRADE P

- Russian Tsar. Kremlin Thug.
- Ex-KGB. Current SOB.
- Slays gays. Arrests rockers.
- Backs hackers. Ally to oligarchs.
- Stalin fan boy.
- *Homo Brutalis* apotheosis.
- Collector of Kompromat.
- Master of the false equivalence.
- The evil, tainted well from which all the world's woes flow.
- Election meddler, both foreign & domestic.
- Shirtless manipulator.
- Law & Order Pipsqueak.

"We shall fight against them, throw them in prisons and destroy them."

-- This was in reference to terrorist insurgents, but you just know this his default reply when asked about anyone he disagrees with.
The New York Times, September 2, 2004.

The Wrong Side of History's
RUSSIAN INVESTMENT

DOLL-HANDS
THE PUPPET

Disclaimer: The following tale is loosely based on certain events.

Once upon a time there lived a corrupt and miserable tyrant named *Comrade P*, mercilessly ruling over a gloomy realm which practiced extreme, cruel capitalism at the expense of its struggling citizenry.

P embarked on an unrelenting quest to re-establish a sphere of influence in Eastern Europe and Central Asia and to return his nation to global power status.

A key component of Comrade P's strategy eventually becomes the weakening of the United States and its democratic allies.

Comrade P needed a big tool to wield in order to implement his sinister schemes of crushing international Democracy and replacing it with pure non-sanctioned, deregulated Oligarchy.

A failed real estate mogul & TV game show emcee massively in debt to Eastern European banks would have to do.

Donny Doll-Hands became the perfect puppet for Comrade P to manipulate and eventually place in a White House that, by 2017, was infested with criminal Deplorables beholden to the whims of this modern Czar & any other two-bit blackmailer in need of quick cash, a sanction lifted or a treaty annulled.

This plot of global domination via corrupt financing was made possible with the willing, eager help and assistance of the characters, businesses, and organizations depicted on these pages.

Comrade P certainly got his ruble's worth.

FELIX SADIST
- Trump family realtor buddy.
- Russian-born dealmaker.
- Originator of the "Trump Tower: Moscow" promise.
- Michael Cohen crony.
- Criminal record:
  - Assault, 1991.
  - Stock fraud, 1998.
- Had KGB connections.
- Trump claimed not to know him.

KUSHY
THE DILETTANTE

MIKEY
THE FIXER

"PRINCESS"
THE SOCIALITE

LUG & IDJIT
- *Fraud Guarantee* guaranteed!
- The *Mafia Rave* club's 2 wild & crazy guys!
- Giuliani's cohorts in conspiracy.
- The Frick & Frack of the Trump-Ukraine scandal.
- A Venn diagram of GOP corruption & dumbness.

RUDY
THE CLOWN

DOOFUS
THE FRONT

CAMBRIDGE ANALYTICA

A-BERT/A-BEKAH
THE FINANCIERS

FACE ZUCK
THE ENABLER

MAGA

P. SPIEL
THE BACKER

PAPADOP
THE COFFEE BOY

SPAM CLOVER
THE AUTHORIZER

LOOSE BANNON
THE AGITATOR

RICK GALOOT
THE FALL GUY

G.R.U.

OAFISH DERPIPASKA
- Putin's oligarch kamerad.
- Made his fortune price gouging raw minerals.
- Das Kapitalist: Extortionist. Racketeer. Briber. Criminal.
- Frivolous SLAPP-er.
- Manafort's sugar daddy who needed a *favor*.
- His net worth "increased" after Jan. 20, 2017.

GUCCIFER 2.0

MARIA BUTTINSKY
- AKA Mata Hari Honeypot.
- NRA's Playmate of the Year.
- The Black Widow of the Red Hat crowd.
- Her love of things phallic was just a false front.
- Blows her cover when blottoed.
- Lots of selfies with *The Wrong Side of History*.
- Avoiding polonium soup back in Moscow.

GALLSTONE
THE MESSENGER

DUMBASS, JR.
THE INBOX

NAUGHTY VASELINEYA
- Magnitsky Act opponent.
- But *HER* emails!
- Schrödinger's attorney: Moscow insider or low-level lackey?
- 2016 appointment book: 6/9 - Trump Tower. Bring "kompromat," blintzes.
- Is she still concerned about those Russian orphans?

PROSKULL
THE PROGRAMMER

WIKILEAKS

NIGEL FOLDEROL
THE ADVISOR

J. ASS ANGER
THE ANARCHIST

RUSSIAN TV

SHILL STEIN
THE DUPE

MAN FORT
THE INFLUENCER

CODGER STAIN
THE RATFUCKER

@RealDonaldTrump September 12, 2013:
Putin's letter is a masterpiece for Russia and a disaster for the U.S. He is lecturing to our President. Never has our Country looked to weak

SERGEY KISSMYASS

- Russia's Ambassador to the U.S. from '08 to '17, until he *wasn't*.
- Trump's 2016 campaign tour groupie turned roadie.
- The Russian with whom:
  - Sessions "didn't" meet.
  - Flynn "didn't" call & chat.
- Kushner's backchannel dropbox.
- Yukking it up in the White House.

FLYNTY — THE COLLUDER

ROSNEFT

SEN. YERTLE — THE TRAITOR

REXXON — THE DEALMAKER

G.O.P.

SHORT SESSIONS — THE COMMUNICATOR

RUSSIABACKER — THE APOLOGIST

CARTER CAGEY — THE SUSPECT

GAZPROM

DEVIN MOO-NES — THE DISTRACTOR

"LOW" BARR — THE OBSTRUCTOR

LINDZEE! — THE PERFORMER

@RealDonaldTrump April 18, 2018:
Slippery James Comey, the worst FBI Director in history, was not fired because of the phony Russia investigation where, by the way, there was NO COLLUSION (except by the Dems)!

BANK OF CYPRUS

"WRINKLES" — THE INVESTOR

PASTOR PENCE — THE BENIGHTED

LURCH LAVATORY

- Russian Minister of ~~Thuggery~~ Foreign Affairs.
- Putin henchman & ideologue.
- Open, dickish disdain toward journalists.
- Trump's 2nd favorite Russian.
- "Recommended" the firing of US intelligence agents (i.e. James Comey).
- AKA "Mr. Nyet."
- Soviet relic.

SCREW N. DOWSKI — THE BULLY

LI'L FLYNTY — THE ASSISTANT

PRINCE BLACKWATER — THE MERCENARY

The Wrong Side of History's
VIRAL MESSAGES

The power & capabilities of the United States' Executive branch are put through the test with how it handles a national emergency. The true character of the President, the administration, and the White House staff, are fully revealed during any crisis that threatens the well-being of the country and, most importantly, its citizens.

Historians can point to various incidents where America was properly lead & inspired to directly tackle a given threat with tenacity, dignity, and determination.

The COVID-19 Pandemic was *NOT* one of those moments.

"We have it very much under control in this country."

-- February 23, 2020

What unfolded was a chaotic collage of how Donny Doll-Hands and his coterie of criminals, capitalists, incompetent careerists, and bureaucratic bunglers hampered and hindered the country's proper recovery from this catastrophic contagion.

Here's a visual flow demonstrating the initial months of the outbreak and how the dumb, greedy & mean hordes prevented credible scientists, reliable civil servants, dedicated care givers, medical pros, and essential workers from properly doing their jobs.

Negligent genocide due to one man's vanity.

RICHARD "INSIDE TRADER" BURR
KELLY "THE SELLER" LOEFFLER

- How to profit off a pandemic without really trying.
- Shared stock info with their family members & campaign investors.

- Abused his position as head of the Senate Intelligence Committee.
- Was he made an example by the DOJ because he didn't sufficiently toady to Trump?

- Doubled down by playing the victim when caught.
- Temporary senator, professional grifter.
- DOJ backed off after husband contributed to Trump campaign.

"I don't take responsibility at all."

-- March 13, 2020

DR. BIRKENSCARF
- Painted ring-around-the-rosie pictures as she wore scarves full of posies.
- Covering for Trump contaminated her career, her rep, & her soul.

DONNY DOLL-HANDS' CORONAVIRUS GUIDELINES FOR AMERICA
DIE SO THE ECONOMY CAN SURVIVE!

"You know, I'm a smart guy. I feel good about it ... You're going to see soon enough. ... We have nothing to lose. You know the expression: What the hell do you have to lose?"
-- March 21, 2020

OFFICIALS ON COUNCIL TO KILL AMERICANS
MAWKISH MEADOWS | "PRINCESS" | KUSHY | THE MUNCHER
LUSHY KUDLOW | ANOTHER WHITE GUY | "WRINKLES" ROSS
FAUX NEWS
LOOK ON MY WORKS, YE MIGHTY, AND DESPAIR! NOTHING BESIDE REMAINS. ROUND THE DECAY OF THAT C

INSTRUCTIONS FOR THE FAUCI FACEPALM*
1. Feel hope drain.
2. Realize how screwed we are.
3. Science-denying assholes are gonna get us all killed.
*Wash your hands before touching your face.

CHANEL RAYON
- Flashy, frivolous fake news fopdoodle.
- Highly coiffed conspiracy crackpot.
- Asks Trump's favorite questions.
- Shitty cartoonist.

ONAN
One Nasty Ass Network

Kushy's PPE National Stockpile
Get your own! (So we can steal it from you)
MINE!

MIKE LINTBALL
- *My Pillow* pillock.
- Crack addict turned smothery, creepy Christian.
- Led unhelpful prayer session at god damn WH press conference.
- The con: Promised to mass produce medical masks. Made cheap cloth ones. Pocketed $75K of tax payer money.
- Trump ego fluffer.

SURGEON JERRY
- Sincerely claimed that Trump was healthier than him. This guy's a doctor?
- Former Indiana state health commissioner, ongoing Mike Pence crony.
- Surgeon General trainee.
- Good at platitudes, bad at solutions.

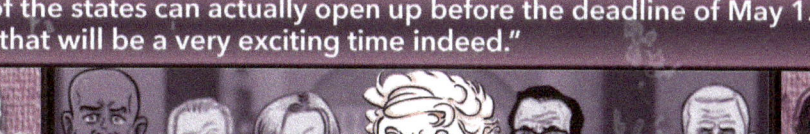
"We think some of the states can actually open up before the deadline of May 1. And I think that that will be a very exciting time indeed."

-- April 15, 2020

@RealDonaldTrump April 17, 2020:
LIBERATE MICHIGAN!

don't cancel MY golf season

COVIDIOTS

THE WALL STREET JOURNAL
OPINION
Do Lockdowns Save Many Lives? In Most Places, the Data Say No
By T.J. Rodgers, founding CEO of Cypress Semiconductor.
Written from the comfort of "most" places: his private estate.
April 26, 2020 *The Wall Street Journal*

Signs: "MY BODY MY CHOICE TRUMP 2020" / "ARBEIT MACHT FREI"

@elonmusk April 29, 2020:
Give people their freedom back!

@elonmusk November 9, 2017:
"If one day, my words are against science, choose science."
--Mustafa Kemal Atatürk

Elon *"Empty Husk"* Musk tweeting from the comfort of his disconnected & contradicting lifestyle.

"We're going to lose anywhere from 75,000, 80,000 to 100,000 people More than 2 million might have died if I hadn't acted to slow the spread. I really believe we have saved a million and a half lives."

-- May 4, 2020

DR. OZDREWPHIL
- The triple-headed guard troll of American quackery & hogwash.
- Pushers of pseudoscience claptrap, hindering pandemic research & info.
- Ready to sacrifice school kids to the herd immunity effect.
- Lockdown blocks their grifty, "snake oil" inspired profit margin.

"I said yesterday we're going to push the pause button here, because I think this whole business of additional assistance for state and local governments needs to be thoroughly evaluated."

-- April 22, 2020.
Senator Yertle Turtle, Champion of the 1%, playing a shell game about *"blue state bailouts,"* adding that states should file for **bankruptcy** instead of receiving **emergency funding**.
His home state of Kentucky netted *more federal cash than 47 other states*, according to the Rockefeller Institute of Government.

@RealDonaldTrump May 9, 2020:
TRANSITION TO GREATNESS!

"I feel like vaccines like I feel about tests. This is going to go away without a vaccine, it's going to go away and we're not going to see it again. There might be flare-ups or maybe not."

Weekly initial unemployment claims in 2020

Sign: "THIS IS A DRY RUN FOR COMMUNISM"

-- May 8, 2020

MOLDY
- Former Acting Secretary of the U.S. Navy.
- Always acting as an asshole.
- Wasted 50 hours of travel & $243K of taxpayer money to insult the reputation of an honorable man whom he fired.
- Rightfully heckled by the crew of the U.S.S. *Theodore Roosevelt*.
- Ended up getting quarantined.

The Wrong Side of History's PUBLIC SERVICE

HEY KIDS! It's **me**! Your **Uncle Billy**! *Dear Leader's* personal fixer/obstructor here to let you know **Operation:Reichstag Fire**, "officially" launched by yours truly, is coming to *a city near you!* We'd appreciate it if all you *agents provocateurs* & *vandalizing troublemakers*, discrediting those BLM activists, got all *riled up 'n' violent* for the cameras. We need to scare Middle America into believing there's a socialist, swarthy, "**Antifa/Defund The Police**" threat to their *God-Fearin' Freedoms!*

Hey! *"Law & Order"* worked in **'68** & **'72** for **Pricky Dick**! That's good enough for **Donny Doll-Hands** in the pandemic year of **2020**! It's all part of our job as *Republicans!* Crushing the surplus population and hoarding power! But we can't win without *cheating!* We've got all sorts of shenanigans planned for **Election Day**! To our *Blue Wave* enemies: Afraid of going to the polls during a *contagious outbreak*? Like your **mail** showin' up on *time*? Live in a predominant urban/ethnic/poor district? Tough break, suckers! I'd say, *"See you in Hell,"* but we're already **there**!

CHUD WOLFENSTEIN
- The DHS's inevitable Made-for-TV fascist enforcer.
- Unqualified at his job, but over-qualified at toadying.
- Bill Barrmy general and GOPstapo director.
- Keeping 'Murica safe from graffiti & the First Amendment.
- Amoral Alpha Moron.
- Clichéd villainy from central casting.

LOUIE DESTROY
- Worthless junk male of the USPS.
- Another wealthy shitbag who wants to whore out a reliable public service for greedy reasons.
- Determined to stamp out Vote-by-Mail during a pandemic.
- Post Disaster General.
- Big donor. Big doofus.
- Got his job C.O.D.
- Sabotaging deliveries like the 1st-Class flunky he is.

Dress rehearsal for Democracy's destruction!
1. Send federal forces to attack peaceful protests.
2. Wait until TV coverage of the resulting chaos spreads.
3. Go on TV to call the chaos a product of "mob violence."
4. Make false arrests to bolster your false narrative.
5. Quietly release those falsely arrested.

STORMTRUMPERS — REAL AMERIKKKAN ACTION FIGURES!

CAPT. JACK BOOT — Liberal cities beware! This unmarked merc's armed with tear gas, a rented van, flash grenades, racism, and non-lethal weapons (wink, wink). Black Lives don't Matter to him! No rights for you, Leftie!

G.I. JOKE — This Boogaloo Boi's done with combat cosplay! He's ready to foment unrest as a U.S. Secret Police agent, bustin' the skulls of unarmed citizens, concerned voters & anyone else who disagrees with his level of "good violence" for the sake of right-wing propaganda.

STUPORSOLDIER — Who better than this stoic, cold, motionless unknown soldier to protect the country's monuments & statues from idealistic, anarchistic Democrats? Hastily trained & mysteriously funded, he won't betray his leaders. Unless you make him a better offer.

THE DONNY DOLL-HANDS MEDIA MANIPULATION SYSTEM

- **INCITE** — A RIOT IS AN UGLY THING & IT'S ABOUT TIME THAT WE HAD ONE!
- **EXPLOIT** — WHATEVER FURTHERS THE BRAND NAME
- **BLAME** — RESPONSIBILITY IS WEAKNESS
- **DISTRACT** — FALSE EQUIVALENCY IS A TRUE FRIEND
- **LIE** — BLATHER, ROUSE, REPEAT

The Wrong Side of History's FUTURE?

The Wrong Side of History's
DISHONORABLE MENTIONS

So many despicable people out there, too many for this book to properly ridicule. Here's an amalgamation of odious crooks, perverts, weirdos, ne'er-do-wells, jerkwads, & creeps deserving of ridicule & scorn, but the constraints of time and the restraints of publishing prevented appropriate placement in the correct context.
A wretched hive of scum and villainy, indeed.

DICKBERT ADAMS

- Social critic/Cartoonist/Asshat.
- Denies: Evolution, The Holocaust, climate change, being human.
- Blames misogyny on women.
- Grifts his fans via unfunny, corporate shilling disguised as libertarian skepticism.
- Self-proclaimed genius sadly searching for relevancy.

ROTTEN AILES

- The fetid father of faux news.
- Media manipulator responsible for 50 years of the worst (i.e. Republican) politicians.
- Old school pervert.
- Went out with a bang, then a whimper.

BASTARD AL-ASSAD

- "President" of Syria. "Friend" of Russia.
- Bush/Cheney would outsource U.S. torture to his capable techniques.
- An adviser to his dad was an actual Nazi.
- Short-sighted authoritarian and ophthalmologist.
- That one side despised by so many in the Syrian civil war clusterfuck.

LAMEASS ALEXANDER

- Key voter on hearing witnesses at Trump's impeachment trial. Cowardly chose "nay" because his comfy retirement was more important.
- Opposed background checks for gun *nuts* buyers.
- Turned a blind eye to the dangers of nuclear energy, but thinks the safer, more efficient, wind turbines are an eyesore.

JIM BILKKER
- Televangelist scam artist.
- Preached conspicuous consumption.
- Hypocritical adulterer.
- Went to jail for fraud. Years later tried to profit from his "redemption."
- Coronavirus cure-all swindler.

JAIR BULLYSCENARIO

- Paranoid, right-wing Brazil nut.
- Yearns for the good ol' days of military dictatorships & banana republics.
- The Tropical Trump.
- Homophobe accusing homosexuals of "heterophobia."
- Villainous arch enemy of the Amazon rain forest.
- Hoisted by his own pandemic petard.

DAN BOMBURSTO

- Carpetbagger extraordinaire.
- Replies to simple questions with profanity-laced tirades & threats.
- Frequent alt-right media guest & substitute host.
- Ex-cop. Ex-Secret Service. *All Lives Matter* apologist.
- Preening blowhard.

WILLIAM F. BUGEYES

- Patriarchal ancestor to America's right-wing.
- Sesquipedalianism show-off.
- Pioneered such modern GOP policies as:
  - Free Market deregulation.
  - Hypocritical drug laws.
  - Support of fascist dictatorships.
  - Bullying, pompous debate tactics.
  - No apologizing for past stupidities.

The Wrong Side of History's
DISHONORABLE MENTIONS

JASON CHAFFING
- Placed all of his political eggs into a worn-out Benghazi basket.
- Wasted legislative capabilities on self-promoting hijinks.
- Cowardly fled his congressional oversight responsibilities in 2017.
- FOX News paycheck ensures his skills at histrionics & deceit won't atrophy.

CHRIS CRISPYCREME
- Low standard politician from a state where "bothsiderism" is a valid argument.
- Water privatization screwed over communities.
- When he's revealed doing the right thing he quickly & cowardly retreats from it.
- *Bridgegate* verified that he burns his political bridges before crossing them.
- Trump taint licker with so many regrets.

JOHNNY CORNHOLE
- Another idiot politician blocking progress.
- Aiding citizens during the pandemic was one big "Blah blah blah" to him.
- Brushes off record high heat waves with frivolous comments, "It's summer…"
- Wallows in revisionist history & unproven conspiracy theories.
- Arrogant concern troll who gets publicly humiliated easily.

BRAGGADOCIO DUTERTE
- Filipino fanatical philistine.
- Brags about a literal body count in which he is gleefully willing to increase.
- An Amnesty International horror show.
- Claims homosexuality is a "disease" & that he was "cured of it." *Okaaaay*.
- He's a rape-y sorta guy. *What a surprise*.
- Drug policy: Zero tolerance, *Holocaust style!*

RANCID ERGOTISM
- Autocratic sultan of Turkey. Power consolidator.
- Armenian Genocide denier who's quick with the "Crimes Against Humanity" accusations.
- Handles peaceful protests with all the subtle diplomacy of a rabid dog.
- Aids & abets terrorist organizations.
- Thin-skinned, litigious asshole who really hates the internet.

J. EDGAR HOSTILE
- Legendary law man/Ugliest transvestite.
- Ran the FBI improperly & illegally for too damn long.
- Believed in the United Surveillance of America.
- Paranoid who equated healthy dissent with pinko COMMUNISM!
- Corrupt cop who denied the existence of organized crime.
- Rabid right-wing racist who ignored such hate groups as the KKK.
- Very easy to blackmail due to his sexual hypocrisy & choice of lingerie.

L-RON HUBBUB
- Bad sci-fi writer, even worse cult leader.
- *Dianetics* unleashed the power of gullibility.
- Started Scientology as a joke. It still is, only the punchline is not "Clear."
- Distrusted psychiatrists, but easily plagiarized from them.
- His official biography myths the mark.
- Fell victim to his own religious dogma.
- The E-Meter is a "stupid people" version of the Voight-Kampff test.

JAMES INAHUFF
- Climate crisis denial nickname: Senator Snowball.
- Member of the Christian fundamentalist, pro-theocracy group *The Fellowship*, a.k.a. *The Family*.
- Made flippant remarks about federal employees & casualties regarding the 1995 Oklahoma City bombing.
- Self-designated arch-enemy of Science.

The Wrong Side of History's
DISHONORABLE MENTIONS

CHAIRMAN X JPEG

- President *For Life* of The "People's" Republic of China. Mao fan boy.
- Opportunistic politician who benefitted from nepotism.
- Anti-corruption campaign: Anyone who threatens his power.
- Ethnic cleansing under a "Chinese Dream" tarp.
- Plays a ping-pong blame game with U.S. re: Crazy COVID-19 Conspiracies.

KRIS KOBOLD

- Kansas' ex-Secretary of State constantly in a state of denial.
- Believes elections are for whites only.
- Having a middle name that started with a "K" would've been pushing it.
- Committed election fraud while searching for evidence of voter fraud.
- No brains or heart, but plenty of nerve.

LOONY LaDOUCHE

- Old school American conspiracist who set the standard for sociocultural paranoia.
- Pioneer of political purity testers & chaos agents.
- 8 failed U.S. Presidential campaigns.
- Self-serving loose cannon. Collected & sold info to ideologically conflicting sides.
- Arrested for mail fraud. Shared a cell with Jim "Bilkker" Bakker.
- Cognitive dissonant cultish con man.

MICHELLE MALIGNANT
- Racist FOX News prop serving as a shield against accusations of racism (Huh?).
- Used when Ann Coulter's not available to screech nutty, hateful, right-wing rhetoric.
- Defended WWII Japanese-American internment camps. Also anti-immigrant.
- Stalks/doxxes children, organizations, & anyone else who publicly displays social empathy/charity.

SWILL MITCHELL

- The title "Internet talk show host" sounds more civilized than "demonic MAGA chud."
- His 2019 *GoFundMe* was a *GoFraudYou*.
- Creepy conspiracist pushing QAnon quackery.
- Lucked into a statistical notoriety that fizzled upon closer inspection. Also, math is hard.
- Declared COVID-19 a "minor infection."
- Denies racism exists 'cuz America allows minorities to earn money.

HORRENDRA MOODI

- Blatant bigot & Hindu nationalist.
- Determined to rewrite India's history by erasing any Islamic references.
- Encourages hate crimes on Muslims.
- Pays trolls to attack/spam any criticism about him on the internet.
- Global conspiracy persecution complex.
- Small, petty man wallowing in ignorance.

JOEL OSTENTATIOUS

- Profit-driven "prophet."
- All the theological nutrition of a circus peanut.
- Popinjay preacher.
- His Megachurch closes during humanitarian crises.
- Views homosexuality as a sin, with an option to condemn.
- Spiritually hollow.

CANDID OFFENCE
- White bigots find her tepidly acceptable.
- Nutty, delusional alt-right commentator.
- Her historical knowledge of Democrats ends before 1960.
- Thinks white supremacy is a "liberal media" myth, & *Black Panther* was a pro-Trump film.
- Charlie "Smirk" Kirk's favorite House Negro.
- Apologist for racists, rapists, and both!
- Belligerent muse for an Australian mass shooter & the Florida MAGA Bomber.

The Wrong Side of History's
DISHONORABLE MENTIONS

WRONG PAUL
- Libertarian Loonytoon.
- Economic crank and fanatical goldbug.
- Political laughingstock.
- Strict constitutionalist whose knowledge of the U.S. Constitution proves he's never read it.
- Difficulties with the whole Church/State separation policy.
- A doctor who mistrusts science.
- His screwy son continues the bad legacy.

JACK POSEURPRICK
- Twerpy Trumpy Troll. *Pizzagate* peddler.
- Hacky blogger who proved it don't take much to be an alt-right darling.
- Punked by the Government of France.
- Got his ass kicked by *Rogue One* and *Captain Marvel*.
- Racist fired by a racist news rag for plagiarizing another racist.
- ~~Exegol~~ OANN accepted him as one of their own (SFX- evil laughter).

JOHN RATFINK
- The Director of National Intelligence's Dunning-Kruger effect.
- Constantly disses the department he's unqualified to lead.
- Pusher of debunked Biden/Ukraine nonsense.
- Incompetent résumé padder.
- Another toady, tool & lying fool.
- Was snuck into the job under cover of pandemic.

JAMOKE ROGAN
- Beliefs, principals & theories based on what he just heard five minutes ago.
- *InfoWars* semi-regular.
- Has spread more lies about COVID-19 faster than bodily fluids at a pool party.
- His populist podcast is an *Experience* of frightened white male privilege.
- Unable to accept change, progress, compassion, and differences.

BEN SENSELESS
- All talk and no action.
- Dutiful GOPer suppressing his humanity for wealth, party loyalty & ignorance.
- Mediocre senator & fake moderate.
- Spineless Trump apologist.
- Believes the poor & the middle class have it too easy, especially during a pandemic.

MATT SCHLUBB
- Churlish chairman of the Awful Caucasians Union (ACU).
- Odious organizer of the Criminals, Parasites, Assholes Conference (CPAC).
- "Threatened" Mitt Romney for daring to vote his conscience.
- Scapegoated other conservatives over CPAC's COVID-19 problem.
- Lobbyist, FOX pundit, goon, lout.

SCOTT WANKER
- Wisconsin's former governor and continual stinky cheesehead.
- Union buster. Teabagger. Kochsucker.
- Willfully ignorant. Easily pranked.
- Eliminated rights to living wages & equal pay.
- Rigged Wisconsin elections to favor Republicans.
- Hindered state job growth.
- Sore loser trying to stay relevant via social media douchebaggery.

JIMMY "CREEPY" WOODS
- Right-wing loudmouth & actor blaming "Hollywood elites" on his fading career.
- Pervs on young girls. Bitches about #MeToo movement.
- Online bully who dishes but can't take it.
- The anger management skills of a strung-out "cocaine addict."
- A homophobic Hades.
- Fired by his agent because 10% of toxic self-destruction is not worth it.

The Wrong Side of History's
FRENEMIES

Politics making strange bedfellows plays on the value of useful allies as long as there are *common enemies*. In an emergency it's never a good choice to turn down assistance because of nit-picky "purity tests," but once the unifying threats have safely passed on to oblivion who's to say progress will be allowed to prosper in ways that will benefit all?

Is there a guarantee that the temporary *comrades-in-arms* won't go back to their self-serving ideologies, encouraging their institutionalized neoconservative *norms* to manufacture another stagnant, wealth-based, "both sides do it" environment, similar to the one that allowed the recent menacing malignancies to flourish and exploit to their advantage?

An *attack dog strategy* against Donny Doll-Hands is much appreciated no matter what the source, but vigilance is a *necessity* since there's an unfortunate precedent with *The Wrong Side of History* to repeat itself.

"MR. KELLYANNE" CONWAY
It's either a ruse to ensure that he (or his wife) has a lucrative post-2020 career, or their hate sex must be *incredible!*

DAVID FRUMP
Axis Of Evil political opportunist who hopes Liberals will ignore his pre-2016 career for the next year or so.

KRISTOL BALL
Chickenhawk pundit who's been wrong for so long that when he says/does the right thing it makes people suspicious.

MITTENS!
The political commitment of an Etch-A-Sketch. But he did that one good thing in a GOP-run Senate. It's the thought that counts.

JENNY RUBE
Neoconservative cosplayer *shocked* that years of Republican talking points resulted in a right-wing monster as President.

STEVE SCHMUTZ
Misses the ol' days ('00-'16) when a "both sides" narrative helped his career. Don't mention Sarah Palin or Howard Schultz to him.

"BEJOE AVERAGE" WALSH
Tea Party racist. Misogynist. Did his "Trump is bad" epiphany activate his *humanity* or his self-preservation mode?

TRICKY WILSON
Lefties with long memories unearthing his rancid behavior & bigoted words are irritants to this *Savior of the Republic*.

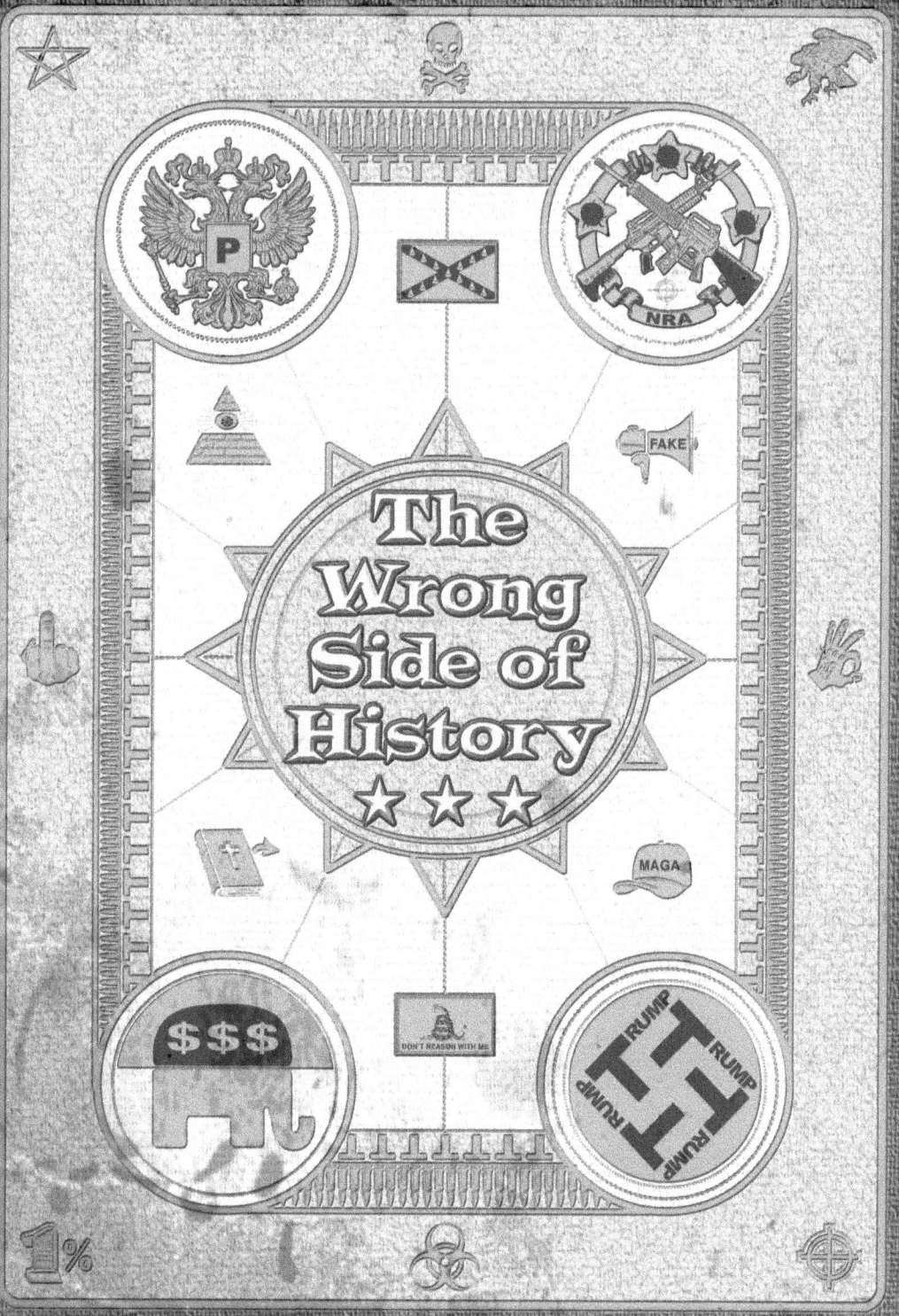

The Wrong Side of History's ACKNOWLEDGEMENTS

- **DailyKos.com & CrooksandLiars.com**
  For news and opinions, duh!

- **Chester Gould's *Dick Tracy***
  The initial visual inspiration for the criminal caricatures. A classic comic strip that depicted true deplorables getting what they deserved.

- **Google.com**
  Yes, the search engine. Made it easy to find all the quote citations and photo references.

- **InvestigateRussia.org**
  All things Trump/Russia. The site that came in handy when the *The Wrong Side of History* memes were starting off on Twitter (@Marlowinc).

- **Mad Magazine**
  The creative combination of illustrations, satire and politics left an early, positive impression on me when I was a kid.

- **MediaMatters.org**
  When I wanted to verify and doublecheck facts on certain people.

- **ProfessionalLeft Podcast with Driftglass & Blue Gal**
  Married journalist bloggers making "both sides" uncomfortable with midwest niceness (professionalleft.blogspot.com).

- **RationalWiki.org**
  A treasure trove of sourced information accented with a satirical bent.

- **Snopes.com**
  Hey! It's Snopes. C'mon!

- **Wikimedia Commons**
  A good source for public domain images (commons.wikimedia.org).

- **Wikipedia.org**
  A helluva lot more trustworthy than WikiLeaks!

The Wrong Side of History's
ACKNOWLEDGEMENTS

Credit/source information regarding the imagery in the *End Times* collage.
Counterclockwise, starting from the top:

- Detail of Christopher Columbus' posthumous portrait, painted by Sebastiano del Plombo 1519.
- *The Purchase of Manhattan Island,* Illustrated by Alfred Fredericks 1909.
- Detail of 1911 advertisement offering "allotted Indian land" for sale.
- Detail of U.S. President Andrew Jackson. 1824 portrait painted by Thomas Sully.
- Photo depicting a 2011 commemoration sign at Big Spring Park, Cedartown, GA describing the Cherokee people's forced march in the Trail of Tears. March 26, 1838.
- Illustration depicting The Marias Massacre of Montana. The slaughter of mostly women and children of the Piegan Blackfeet tribe. January 23, 1870. Artist unknown.
- Public notice of slave auction. May 18, 1829.
- Woodcut print depicting a slave patrol capturing a fugitive slave. From the abolitionist Anti-Slavery Almanac (1839).
- Print portrait of Confederate Army General Robert E Lee. 1864. Photographer Julian Vannerson. U.S. Library of Congress.
- Men and boys pose beneath the body of Lige Daniels, a black man, shortly after he was lynched on August 3, 1920, in Center, Texas. This horrific scene was printed on postcards.
- Bloody Sunday - Alabama police attack Selma-to-Montgomery Marchers, March 1965.
- Video frame of Los Angeles police beating the unarmed Rodney King taken by witness George Holliday. Timecode date: March 3, 1991.
- Video frame of Minneapolis State Police Officer Derek Chauvin murdering George Flloyd taken by witness/bystander Darnella Frazier May 25, 2020.
- The torture of Abu Ghraib prisoner Abdou Hussain Saad Faleh by US Army and CIA personnel. Iraq 2003.
- Still frame taken from video of former Saudi Arabian socialite and CIA-trained Afghani freedom fighter turned international bad guy, Osama bin Laden, threatening more blowback on the West. Circa 2001.
- Vietnam War protest poster "Nixon's Peace." Circa 1969. Based on a design by Félix Beltrán.
- "Tail-Gunner Joe" McCarthy, Roy Cohn's boozy partner in slander, during a quiet, paranoid reverie. 1954. U.S. Library of Congress.
- Joseph Stalin, Putin's ideological muse, enjoying his pipe during a quiet moment from all the carnage. 1937.
- Photos *Holocaust* and *Arbeit Mach Frei.* 1945. United States Holocaust Memorial Museum (ushmm.org).
- Benito Mussolini, Italian fascist & fashion junkie. The Curly to Hitler's Moe. 1930.
- Nostradamus' second antichrist, no doubt spouting something racist in German. Circa 1930s.
- Image of a woodcut depicting the unfortunate victims of the Salem Witch Trials. Circa early 17th century.
- Image of a woodcut depicting waterboarding included in J. Damhoudère's Praxis Rerum Criminalium, Antwerp. 1556.

The Wrong Side of History's ADDENDUM

Life doesn't stop between the composition of a "current events" book and a publication date.

BRAD PROSKULL-
Incompetency, embezzlement & canoodling with Hope Hexxed got him demoted as Donny Doll-Hands' 2020 "re-election" campaign manager. The guy "knew too much" to be fired.

MATT PUTZ-
A sudden, unexpected, and questionable parentage. #FreeNestor.

TOMMY ROTTEN-
Dangerous attempts to make himself relevant to right-wingers by championing authoritarian measures. The man has Presidential ambitions and needs to be stopped. He's Donny Doll-Hands with sinister intelligence.

STEVE KKKING-
Lost the 2020 Republican primary in Iowa, ensuring his time in the U.S. Congress was over. Granted, his opponent was just as bad, only less quiet about it by comparison.
"Some people say" that KKKing will probably fail sideways toward a paid pundit position and may be considered a "consultant" on right-wing media.

WAYNE LAPARIAH-
The New York Attorney General discovered that Wayne and his buddies have been committing all sorts of criminal shenanigans at the Nutjobs • Relics • Assholes club. A lawsuit has been filed to dissolve this domestic terrorist organization. Thoughts & prayers!

REV. PATRONIZE-
Publicly chastised Doll-Hands about his use of the military to suppress protestors demonstrating their 1st Amendment rights to assemble. This one act of concern doesn't make up for the preacher's terrible history, but it does put a blemish on Donny's evangelical support.

FALLINHELL-
Apparently, Junior had some wardrobe malfunction that went viral on social media. The oh-so-pious people at Liberty University, having lost their tolerance of such scandals, sent their founder's son on a forced sabbatical.

ABOUT THE AUTHOR

ROBERT KEOUGH

- Unemployable illustrator.
- Humorist who laughs at his own jokes.
- Curmudgeon. Misanthrope.
- A head full of useless trivia.
- Wastes his days being antisocial on social media.
- Hawking stuff online.
- So tired & fed up with The Wrong Side of History.

www.marlowinc.com

"I can't get enough out of my *Donny Doll-Hands* travel mug and other fine *Wrong Side of History* products! It's treasonably good!"

Thanks for the plug, "Princess"!